CAMBRIDGE
UNIVERSITY PRESS

CAMBRIDGE
Language Assessm
Part of the University of Camb

# Cambridge English

Niki Joseph
Series Editor: Annette Capel

# Prepare!
## WORKBOOK
### Level 5

**Cambridge University Press**
www.cambridge.org/elt

**Cambridge English Language Assessment**
www.cambridgeenglish.org

Information on this title: www.cambridge.org/9781107497870

© Cambridge University Press and UCLES 2015

First published 2015
3rd printing 2015

Printed in Italy by Rotolito Lombarda S.p.A.

*A catalogue record for this publication is available from the British Library*

ISBN 978-1-107-48234-0 Student's Book
ISBN 978-1-107-49793-1 Student's Book and Online Workbook
ISBN 978-1-107-49792-4 Student's Book and Online Workbook with Testbank
ISBN 978-1-107-49787-0 Workbook with Audio
ISBN 978-1-107-49788-7 Teacher's Book with DVD and Teacher's Resources Online
ISBN 978-1-107-49786-3 Class Audio CDs
ISBN 978-1-107-49789-4 Presentation Plus DVD-ROM

Downloadable audio for this publication at www.cambridge.org/PrepareAudio

# Contents

1   Going shopping                        4

2   Friends forever                       8

3   Fun and games                        12

4   From fire to snow                    16

5   You made it!                         20

6   Take good care of yourself           24

7   Sound checks                         28

8   Amazing architecture                 32

9   The future is now                    36

10  Animals and us                       40

11  Off to school                        44

12  Getting around                       48

13  Perfect or real?                     52

14  Ready to cook                        56

15  City and countryside                 60

16  Let's film that!                     64

17  Getting the message                  68

18  We love the celebs!                  72

19  The world of work                    76

20  Making plans                         80

# 1 Going shopping

## VOCABULARY  Shopping

**1** Match the words to their meanings.

1 change ......
2 charge ......
3 discount ......
4 online shopping ......
5 receipt ......
6 refund ......
7 send something back ......
8 serve ......
9 shop ......
10 spend ......

a a piece of paper you receive when you buy something
b money given back to you if you return something
c take something back to a shop and replace it with something else
d buy things
e help customers in a shop
f ask for money for a service or activity
g use money to buy or pay for something
h shopping on the internet
i return an item that you bought online
j a lower price than usual for something

**2** Choose the correct answer.

1 I paid for the book with a €20 note and the assistant gave me €4 *change / charge*.
2 I saw an advertisement yesterday about a 20% *refund / discount* on all electrical items.
3 If the shorts don't fit, you can always *send them back / refund them*.
4 How much did you *shop / spend* on that new game?
5 I've lost the *refund / receipt* but perhaps you have the information on your computer system.
6 When you work in a shop, you have to do more than just *serve / charge* customers.
7 Maisy and her friend love to *shop / spend* for clothes in M&F.
8 The watch shop doesn't *charge / spend* you if you need a new battery.
9 The sales assistant said that I could get a *receipt / refund* if I brought the jumper back within 30 days.
10 You can sometimes get the clothes you want at a much cheaper price when you use *online shopping / discounts*, and the shops usually deliver too!

**3** Complete the sentences with the words in the box. There are two words you do not need.

> change    charge    discounts    online
> receipt    refund    served    spend

1 The shop gave me a ........................... for my t-shirt.

2 Get to Booksforall now! We have amazing ...........................!

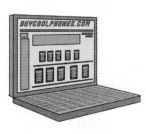

3 Have you ever done any ........................... shopping?

4 The boy who ........................... us is in Year 12.

5 We sometimes have to pay a delivery ........................... .

6 Monica got a ........................... on those jeans.

**4** Complete the sentences so that they are true for you.

1 I spend about ........................... on clothes per month
2 I love shopping for ........................... but I hate shopping for ........................... .
3 In my country, they charge us to go into ........................... .
4 The last thing that I sent back was ...........................

# READING

**1** Quickly read about Matt and Annika's shopping experiences. Who might buy these things? Write M or A.

books ☐   clothes ☐   food ☐   school bag ☐   second-hand goods ☐

*st month we invited you
send in your photos and
cles about the last place
u shopped. We decided
rint these two answers
Matt and Annika. How
different!*

I really like going round the markets with my friends. There are markets on the first Sunday of the month near my house. They sell lots of different things. The market is divided up into different areas so for example there's the food area. You can't miss it because there's a big sign above the entrance. You can do your weekly grocery shopping, you know, fruit and vegetables, or you can just have a coffee and a piece of cake there. Then there's the clothes section, which my sister loves but I think is really boring. I mean, clothes are clothes! One thing I like best about the market is the second-hand goods area – that's where you can find anything and everything! There are old books, furniture, kitchen equipment and some really amazing objects. The other week I found a really old paperweight; you use it to stop papers from blowing away. It's made of heavy glass and it's beautiful because you can see different colours in it. I think it's an antique. But I think the best part is the entertainment. There's always someone playing some music. It's such a great atmosphere.
*Matt, aged 15*

I think the last time I bought something was online. I generally buy all my clothes online these days. It's so much easier and it's really convenient. Also, you can get all the latest fashions from Europe. Here in New Zealand we have to wait for ages for things to come from Europe into the shops. I think it's because we are so far away and our winter is in the European summer. But now with online shopping, it doesn't matter. I have several apps that are looking out for what I want. At the moment, I've got an app searching for a cool school bag that I saw online. Of course, I have to look out for delivery charges! But I usually manage to get some great discounts. I think that's the great thing about technology and it's definitely made a difference for those of us who live a long way away!
*Annika, aged 16*

**2** Read the article again and answer these questions.

1 When is the market near Matt's house?
.................................................................

2 What is Matt's favourite part of the market?
.................................................................

3 What did he buy there? And what is it used for?
.................................................................

4 What adds to the atmosphere of the market in Matt's opinion?
.................................................................

5 What does Annika buy online?
.................................................................

6 Why does she say that fashions can take a long time to get to New Zealand?
.................................................................

7 How does she find her items?
.................................................................

8 What is she looking for at the moment?
.................................................................

**EP Word profile** *thing*

Complete the sentences with a phrase from the box. You need to use one phrase twice.

> a thing    that kind of thing    the thing
> the same thing    things like that

1 Mark says that there isn't ............................. on TV tonight.
2 ............................. I like about Sarah is that she's always happy.
3 I spent the weekend tidying my room, watching TV, you know, ............................. .
4 I lost my favourite pen and I've got another one but it isn't ............................. .
5 When you visit me, we'll do some sports, like swimming and ............................. .
6 ............................. with smartphones is that they use a lot of battery.

# GRAMMAR  Determiners

**1**  **Choose the correct word.**

1  Last week my parents visited ....... shops.
   a  no      b  any      c  several

2  They wanted to buy ....... computer games for my brother and me.
   a  much      b  some      c  plenty

3  There are so ....... games to choose from.
   a  much      b  many      c  a lot of

4  They asked the shop assistant ....... questions.
   a  any      b  plenty      c  a lot of

5  He told them that ....... two games are exactly the same.
   a  much      b  no      c  many

6  He said that there weren't ....... action games in the shop at the moment.
   a  plenty      b  several      c  any

7  There was an animal game, but he didn't think it would be ....... fun for me.
   a  no      b  much      c  many

8  But then they looked online and they found ....... of games to choose from.
   a  plenty      b  several      c  some

**2**  **Complete the conversation with the words from the box.**

> a lot of   any   many   much   no
> plenty   several   some   some

**A:** Hi! Can I help you?

**B:** Yes, I'd like ¹ ....................... information about an extra piece of equipment I need for my mobile phone.

**A:** OK, which one? We have ² ....................... extras here!

**B:** My friend said that there are ³ ....................... batteries that last a long time between charging them. I have a battery at the moment but it doesn't last ⁴ ....................... time at all.

**A:** Well, it depends what you do. ⁵ ....................... battery lasts forever!

**B:** No, I know, but my friend said it gives ⁶ ....................... charges.

**A:** Ah, I know. It's called a power box, I think. I've got them in ⁷ ....................... of different colours.

**B:** That's it. How ⁸ ....................... power does it have?

**A:** I think it has three charges in it. I have a more expensive model that has ⁹ ....................... more charges – about 20 I think.

**B:** No, I think that three is enough. Thanks! I'll take it!

**3**  **Choose the correct sentence in each pair.**

1  a  Do you have free time on Saturday?
   b  Do you have any free time on Saturday?

2  a  My mum bought a lot of clothes and some snacks for me.
   b  My mum bought many clothes and some snacks for me.

3  a  My brother likes very much sport.
   b  My brother likes sport very much.

4  a  I have so much shoes!
   b  I have so many shoes!

5  a  I know that you will enjoy it a lot.
   b  I know that you will enjoy it too much.

# VOCABULARY  any

**1**  **Match the questions to the answers.**

1  Where are my shoes?  .......
2  How are you feeling today?  .......
3  What's the matter with your phone?  .......
4  Did you get Mark's present?  .......
5  Can I borrow that, please?  .......
6  Where's Marcia?  .......
7  Why was he shouting at you?  .......

a  I have no idea. I haven't done anything wrong.
b  No, there wasn't anything suitable.
c  This app isn't any good.
d  I haven't seen them anywhere.
e  I don't know. I haven't seen her anywhere.
f  You can have it! I don't want it any more.
g  Not any better really.

**2**  **Choose the correct answer.**

1  I haven't made *anything / any good* for dinner yet.

2  Emily Johnson isn't at our school *any more / any good*. She moved last term.

3  This film isn't *any more / any good* – let's watch something different.

4  Has *anyone / any* got a pen?

5  There isn't *anything / anywhere* in the fridge. Can we go out for dinner?

6  My test results this term weren't *any better / any good* than last term.

7  Leonardo Di Caprio still hasn't won *any / anything* Oscars.

8  I don't mind where we go – *anywhere / anything* away from here!

# WRITING  Notes

**1** Read the notes and complete the table below.

> Hi Mum,
>
> Here's the battery that doesn't work. Can you take it back to the store for me and exchange it for a new one please? The receipt is in the bag with it.
>
> Thanks,
>
> Sam.

> Dad,
>
> The book is in my bedroom. There are four pages missing, as I told you yesterday (pages 4–7). It would be great if you could get a refund. I can't find the receipt anywhere but the shop assistant's name was Becka.
>
> Phil

> Angelina,
>
> Here's my pencil case. When you go to the supermarket, can you take it and tell them that it doesn't close properly. I think it's broken. I only bought it yesterday so I don't think it'll be a problem. The receipt is inside it. Can you get me a new one — any colour will do!
>
> Thanks,
>
> Max

| Name | Object | What to do |
|------|--------|------------|
| Sam |  |  |
|  | book |  |
|  |  | get a new one |

**2** Read these sentences from another note. Number them in the correct order.

a  See you later, ☐

b  I won't be home until six tonight. ☐

c  Here's some money. ☐

d  Hi Josh, ☐

e  Mum ☐

f  Can you go to the shops and get some lasagne for supper? ☐

**3** Here are two more notes but the sentences are mixed up. Write the two notes. Put your name at the end.

Can you take it in to the phone store today?

Can you see if they have it in black, please?

Do you remember the red shirt I bought last week?

Remember to find out when it will be back!

Here's my mp3 player.

Hi Susie,

I'm a size M.

Rob,

Thanks

Thanks

The screen doesn't work.

When you go to town, can you go in the clothes shop?

> Hi Susie,
>
> ............................................................
> ............................................................
> ............................................................
> ............................................................
> ............................................................
> ............................................................
> ............................................................

> Rob,
>
> ............................................................
> ............................................................
> ............................................................
> ............................................................
> ............................................................
> ............................................................
> ............................................................

**4** You bought something from a local shop but you decide you don't want it. Write a note to your father.

- Say what you bought.
- Say why you don't want it any more.
- Ask him to take it back and ask for a refund.

## VOCABULARY   Personality adjectives

**1** Complete the crossword, using the clues below.

**Across**

This describes someone who …
1  doesn't give much thought to things.
3  you can trust.
4  is always calm and doesn't worry.
8  makes you feel angry.
9  tells the truth.

**Down**

This describes someone who …
1  likes being with people.
2  isn't kind.
5  learns quickly.
6  is sure of their ability.
7  makes good decisions.
8  worries about things.

**2** Choose the correct answer.

1  Susie always tells you what she really thinks.
   She's *honest / intelligent*.
2  I don't like the way Josh talks to Ben. I think he's
   quite *anxious / cruel*.
3  Jake studied really hard for the test and he was
   *confident / silly*.
4  My friend is *annoying / reliable* because he
   keeps changing the date of his party.
5  Yesterday we laughed so much about tiny things –
   we were really *silly / talented*.
6  My test is tomorrow and I feel *anxious / reliable*
   because I haven't studied.
7  Duncan is never calm or relaxed – certainly not
   *easygoing / annoying*.
8  Frank is a *silly / reliable* student – he'll bring in
   the note from his mum tomorrow.

**3** Choose a word from the box to describe each teen.

> confident   easygoing   honest   intelligent
> reliable   sensible   sociable   talented

I make sure I do something when I say I'll do it.

1  ..............................

I always take my phone with me so that I can call home if necessary.

2  ..............................

I'm not worried about winning – it's going to be easy!

3  ..............................

I love hanging out with friends and being with people.

4  ..............................

I don't mind which film we see – both are probably good.

5  ..............................

I don't have to study too much at the moment. Schoolwork is all quite easy for me.

6  ..............................

I'm lucky because it isn't hard for me to draw pictures of people.

7  ..............................

If I find some money in the school, I take it to the head teacher.

8  ..............................

# READING

**1** Read the title of the article and write three ideas to answer it. Then read the article quickly. Are your ideas there?

1 .......................................................................
2 .......................................................................
3 .......................................................................

## EXAM TIPS

**Reading Part 3**
- First, read the text quickly to get a general idea of what it is about.
- Read the sentences and then read the text again. The sentences are in the same order as the information in the text.
- Underline the parts of the text that tell you whether each sentence is correct or incorrect.

# WHAT DOES IT MEAN TO BE A FRIEND?

This is what happened to Kennedy. It was break time and she was chatting with her friends when this boy ran round the corner really fast and went straight into her. She put her hand to her mouth and noticed some blood. The boy said it was her fault – that was horrible! Her friend, Rachel, wasn't afraid of arguing with the boy. She immediately shouted, 'No, you're wrong. I saw everything!'

It can be challenging to find true friendship, but Kennedy recognised it – and so did many of you. We asked for your opinions and ideas about true friendship. You sent us over 100,000 replies!

For many, what you *do* for a friend is more important than what you *say*. Denise writes about a friend who admitted to something that she didn't do. It was all about a silly drawing of a teacher. Her friend had to go to the head teacher's office and got extra homework. Was she sensible? Probably not, but she was a good friend.

It's not just what your friends do for you, though; it's what you do for them. Gary remembers the time he was at football practice and his friend really wanted to be in the team. 'I told the teacher I was going away at the weekend. I wasn't honest but my friend got a place in the team.'

However, there's one thing you don't agree about: how many best friends can you have? Molly says she has one best friend and all her other friends are 'close'. Kaitlyn, 14, says it depends on your age. 'When I was younger, I was interested in having lots of best friends. But now I have just one best friend.' But that's the girls: what about the boys? Well, it seems that you generally have lots of friends but you don't worry about best friends, or close friends. You just have … *friends*.

**2** 🔵 Read the sentences below. Read the article again and decide if each sentence is correct or incorrect. If it is correct, write A. If it is not correct, write B.

1 Kennedy hurt a boy by accident at school. .......
2 Her friend Rachel was too scared to talk to the boy about what happened. .......
3 The magazine asked readers to write in with their thoughts about friendship. .......
4 Denise's friend said she drew a silly picture of a teacher. .......
5 Gary told his games teacher the truth. .......
6 Kaitlyn has several best friends at the moment. .......

**3** Match the highlighted words in the text to the meanings.

1 difficult ...............................
2 feel anxious about ...............................
3 answers ...............................
4 know something or someone because you have seen it before ...............................
5 a red liquid in your body ...............................

**EP Word profile** *close*

**Match the dialogue halves.**

1 Tell me about your friends. .......
2 Do the shops always close at 5 pm? .......
3 Where's your school? .......
4 Have you just opened the window? .......
5 Do you know this author? .......

a No, they are open later on Thursdays.
b Yes, she's a close relative.
c Yes, it was closed and it's hot in here.
d Jenny and Rob are my close friends.
e It's the building closest to the park on the left.

# GRAMMAR  -ing forms

**1** Complete the sentences with the -ing form of the verb in brackets.

1 The teacher doesn't mind ............................ (describe) the rules again.

2 My friend Nathan enjoys ............................ (run) early in the morning with his dad.

3 Some young teens can't stand ............................ (drink) coffee.

4 Zoe considered ............................ (do) her maths homework before dinner.

5 The design teacher suggested ............................ (make) the box from wood.

6 Yvonne imagined ............................ (say) hello to her new friend.

7 I didn't believe Liam when he said he was sorry; he isn't very good at ............................ (lie) to his friends.

8 Sally always stays on the beach when we go to the seaside because she hates ............................ (swim) in the sea.

**2** Write sentences. Use the correct form of the verbs.

0 Julia / love / make / a big breakfast for her parents.
   *Julia loves making a big breakfast for her parents.*

1 Mikey / can't stand / go / food shopping.
   ......................................................................

2 Bob / not really like / watch / horror films.
   ......................................................................
   ......................................................................

3 Jade / enjoy / write letters / to her friends.
   ......................................................................
   ......................................................................

4 Morgan / like / play / basketball / with his friends after school.
   ......................................................................
   ......................................................................

5 Philippa / not mind / stay / home alone.
   ......................................................................
   ......................................................................

6 Harry / very keen on / study / something different / every year.
   ......................................................................
   ......................................................................

7 Maria / can't / imagine / leave / home / and live / on her own.
   ......................................................................
   ......................................................................

8 Jordan / doesn't enjoy / shop / with his sisters.
   ......................................................................
   ......................................................................

**3** Match the adjectives to the prepositions.

| 1 | afraid | ............................ | **a** | on |
| 2 | good | ............................ | **b** | at |
| 3 | keen | ............................ | **c** | in |
| 4 | crazy | ............................ | **d** | about |
| 5 | interested | ............................ | **e** | of |

**4** Complete the text with a preposition from A and a verb from B. Use the -ing form of the verb.

Ⓐ | about   at   in   of   on |

Ⓑ | catch   do   have   play   walk |

My friends and I are interested [1] ............................ the same things. We are all really crazy [2] ............................ the same sports. We're all keen [3] ............................ a game of basketball together whenever we can – even the ones who aren't very good [4] ............................ the ball. Sometimes we play for hours and finish very late and Mum doesn't like it! She collects me because she knows I'm afraid [5] ............................ home in the dark on my own.

**5** Ⓞ Correct the mistakes in these sentences or put a tick (✔) by any you think are correct.

1 I'm writting to you because I want to answer your questions. ............................

2 Please let me know whether you go or not.
   ............................

3 I thought about going to the concert.
   ............................

4 I hope you will enjoy play it. ............................

5 We like doing homework or studing together.
   ............................

6 What do you like doing with your friends?
   ............................

## VOCABULARY   Prefixes: *un-* and *dis-*

**1** Write the negative form of the <u>underlined</u> word.

1 I thought our teacher was <u>kind</u> when he gave us extra homework. ............................

2 This room smells <u>pleasant</u>. ............................

3 You were really <u>lucky</u> with that question. ............................

4 I <u>agree</u> with you. ............................

5 Zak suddenly <u>appeared</u> at the party. ............................

6 This programme is so <u>interesting</u>. Let's watch something else. ............................

7 Maria looked quite <u>happy</u> this morning. What's wrong? ............................

8 I really <u>like</u> this kind of TV programme. ............................

**2** Complete the conversations with one of these adjectives, or its negative form.

> agree   happy   interesting   kind   like   lucky

1 **A:** I don't think we have enough homework – we need more at the weekend.
  **B:** I ............................ with you!

2 **A:** I loved reading this book.
  **B:** Me too! It was really ............................ .

3 **A:** I love my friends.
  **B:** Same here! We're so ............................ to be friends.

4 **A:** Do you really like maths?
  **B:** No, I really ............................ it. It's difficult and I don't understand it.

5 **A:** Do you know what's wrong with Maggie?
  **B:** Well, I know she's ............................ but I don't know why.

6 **A:** Did you meet my friend Nick?
  **B:** Yes, he's lovely and he said some really ............................ things about you.

## LISTENING

**1** You will hear an English teacher talking about a homework project. Tick (✔) the topics you think he's going to talk about.

what the homework is about ☐
what last year's group did ☐
how many words it should be ☐
examples of what he wants / doesn't want ☐
his own ideas on the subject ☐
when he wants the homework ☐

**2** ▶2 Listen and check your answers.

## EXAM TIPS

**Listening Part 3**
• Look at the six spaces in the notes before you listen.
• Decide what kind of information is missing.
• Think of possible answers.

**3** Look at the notes in exercise 4. What can you put in the spaces?

|  | **Space** |
| --- | --- |
| nouns | ............................ |
| adjectives | ............................ |

**4** ▶2 ● Listen again. For each question, fill in the missing information. Use no more than two words.

> ### ARTICLE ABOUT ONLINE FRIENDS
>
> an article for a **(1)** ............................ magazine.
>
> *Ideas:*
>
> how **(2)** ............................ is changing our friendships
>
> Are online friends nice or do they make unpleasant **(3)** ............................ ?
>
> a **(4)** ............................ of an event with a friend
>
> What **(5)** ............................ do your online friends have?
>
> how long online **(6)** ............................ last

**5** Match the questions to the answers.

1 What's your name? How do you spell it? .......
2 Where are you from? .......
3 What's your house like? .......
4 Do you play sports? .......
5 When do you go to bed? .......
6 Do you read books? Why? / Why not? .......

a It's quite big, with a garden at the back.
b Quite early, at about 10 pm, because I like to get up early.
c I do, but only once or twice a week at school.
d It's Bouvier. That's B-O-U-V-I-E-R.
e Yes, all the time. I love reading, especially adventure stories.
f Quebec, that's in the French part of Canada.

# ③ Fun and games

## VOCABULARY  Sports phrases

**1** Write the letters in the correct order to make verbs. Write them on the short lines.

0 NEETR ......*enter*......
...*a competition/tournament*...

1 VIEG ........................
........................

2 ONJI ........................
........................

3 SISM ........................
........................

4 TEAB ........................
........................

5 SOEL ........................
........................

6 NIW ........................
........................

7 AHEV ........................
........................

8 CSOER ........................
........................

**2** Write the phrases from the box under the verbs in exercise 1.

> a club/gym    ~~a competition/tournament~~
> a go    a goal/point    a game/match
> a prize/medal/game/match
> (someone) the chance
> the opportunity    the other team

**3** Chose the correct answer.

1 Jake *entered* / *gave* a competition.
2 Maria's team *scored* / *won* a goal.
3 This year I *missed* / *gave* the opportunity to do scuba diving.
4 The captain *joined* / *gave* me the chance to play in goal.
5 The Jones family have *had* / *joined* a gym – they want to get fit.
6 David is sad because his team *lost* / *entered* the match.
7 During our activity week, you can *have* / *give* a go at lots of different sports.
8 At the end of the tournament, I *won* / *join* a prize – I came first!
9 We *won* / *beat* the other team 4–0!

**4** Complete the captions with verbs and nouns from exercise 1.

1 Look at Sam!
He's ........................ .

2 My dad ........................
last week!

3 Oh dear! How did we
........................ ?

4 Hurray! We ........................
the other ........................ .

**5** Mark has had some ideas to raise money through sport. Write complete sentences.

1 In our football match / everyone / give some money / when we score / goal
........................................................................
........................................................................

2 Everyone who / enter / tournament / next week / have to pay / €5.00
........................................................................
........................................................................

3 Every time / we / have / go / at a new sport / we / give / some money to charity
........................................................................
........................................................................

4 If we / win / all / our matches / the other teams / give / money / to our club
........................................................................
........................................................................

http://thingsiminterestedin.wordpress.com     🔍 Search

| upload pictures | reblog | tag | comment |

I've just read a blog about volunteers in sports and I thought I'd write about it. We all know how important sport is but did you know that volunteers in sport are also really important? I had no idea! For example, most of the coaches and managers are volunteers. Without them, many sporting champions simply wouldn't be a champion.

Have you heard of the Australian rower Kim Crow? She's won a lot of prizes including silver and bronze medals at the London 2012 Olympics. So what, you're probably thinking. Well, she's also a lawyer, with a full-time job! Many people think that sportspeople train or compete all day but they don't. They have normal jobs and they train in their free time.

In addition, Kim Crow also works as a volunteer. She gives presentations, goes into schools and talks to kids about the importance of exercise, and of course she teaches teens how to row. So she takes the skills that she has learnt and gives them back. Also, when there's a race day, she sometimes asks people if they can help out. I didn't realise until the other day that the helpers are all volunteers at these races. You know, I honestly thought everyone was just doing a job. Well, I guess they are, but they just don't get paid. It provides them with the opportunity to see the race, but they also make it happen.

It seems that sports like rowing can't happen without volunteers. But super Kim doesn't help with just one organisation – she does several different projects at the same time! She likes that because of the variety and she's happy to give something back. At the moment she's trying to get other top athletes to help run sporting sessions every fortnight for all groups in the community. I read about people like her and I have so much respect. I think that everyone should have a go at being a volunteer. You help other people and you help yourself.

About me

Archive
January (2)

Blogroll
http://thingsiliketodo.
blogspot.com

This blog has 398 followers.  Follow this blog.

# READING

**1 Read David's blog and answer the questions.**

1 Who is Kim Crow?

.................................................................

2 Why does David respect her?

.................................................................

**2 Read the blog again and answer the questions.**

1 What surprises David in the first paragraph?

.................................................................

2 What does Kim Crow do? (three things)

.................................................................

.................................................................

.................................................................

3 What activities with young people does Kim do?

.................................................................

.................................................................

4 What did David discover recently about boat races?

.................................................................

5 What is she organising at the moment?

.................................................................

.................................................................

**3 Match the highlighted words in the text to the meanings.**

1 talks giving information about something    .........................

2 people who teach a sport    .........................

3 a lot of different types of things    .........................

4 a period of two weeks    .........................

5 a person, animal or team that wins a competition    .........................

6 happening or working for the whole of the working week    .........................

**EP** **Word profile** *give*

**Match the questions to the replies.**

1 Do you know the answer?   .......

2 When's the homework for?   .......

3 Is dinner ready yet?   .......

4 What was your best birthday present?   .......

5 Why do you like the library so much?   .......

a Give me another ten minutes, guys!

b Mum gave me an awesome pair of trainers.

c It gives you the chance to learn, and be somewhere quiet.

d No, I give in!

e We have to give it in by next Tuesday.

**Fun and games**    13

## GRAMMAR Present simple and continuous

**1** Make sentences about the pictures, using the words under each one.

**0** I / have / lots of fun!

...I'm having lots of fun!...

**1** Nancy / run / the same route / every morning

........................................................................

........................................................................

**2** We / do / our homework / for tomorrow

........................................................................

........................................................................

**3** I / stay / with my sister / for the weekend

........................................................................

........................................................................

**4** All cameras / work / in a similar way / I / think

........................................................................

........................................................................

**2** Are the <u>underlined</u> verbs in these sentences correct or incorrect? Correct them if necessary.

**1** I<u>'m talking</u> to my friends on
Facebook at the moment.          ...........................

**2** Dad <u>is playing</u> golf with his friends
every Saturday morning.          ...........................

**3** By ten o'clock most evenings,
I<u>'m feeling</u> tired and ready for bed.  ...........................

**4** Tess <u>is having</u> a picnic with her
friend Jenny tomorrow.          ...........................

**5** Does anyone know how this app
<u>is working</u>?                  ...........................

**6** Mum never <u>gets</u> the train to work –
she says it's too slow!          ...........................

**7** The Earth <u>is going round</u> the Sun.  ...........................

**3** Complete the conversation with the correct form of the verbs in the box.

> do    fix    have    install    meet
> (not) know    want    (not) work

**Anna:** What ¹ ........................... at the moment, Fred?

**Fred:** Oh, you know, things. Nothing special really,
although I ² ........................... Martin in town at
five. Why?

**Anna:** Well, my other phone ³ ...........................
properly and I ⁴ ........................... you to look
at it.

**Fred:** Oh, OK, but I ⁵ ........................... much about
phones.

**Anna:** But you ⁶ ........................... Mike's phone,
aren't you? That's what he said!

**Fred:** No, I ⁷ ........................... a program –
it's different.

**Anna:** Oh, OK. I'll think of something. See you
at home later – we ⁸ ...........................
pancakes for dinner! Don't be late!

**Fred:** Oh, yum! See you later, sis.

**4** 👁 Choose the correct sentence in each pair.

**1 a** I write you this email to invite you to a party.
  **b** I'm writing you this email to invite you to a party.

**2 a** Every Friday and Saturday we are going to the
cinema and we have a lot of fun!
  **b** Every Friday and Saturday we go to the cinema
and we have a lot of fun!

**3 a** We play football very often and in the past we
were in the same football club.
  **b** We're playing football very often and in the past
we were in the same football club.

**4 a** I'm sending this email because I have a new
computer game.
  **b** I send this email because I have a new computer
game.

## VOCABULARY   Strong adjectives and adverbs

**1** Write the letters in the correct order to make strong adjectives, then write the normal adjectives from the box next to them.

> bad   big   cold   old   tired

1 STAUDEEXH ........................ ........................
2 NANCTIE ........................ ........................
3 ORNOMSUE ........................ ........................
4 ETIRRELB ........................ ........................
5 ZERENFIG ........................ ........................

**2** Choose the correct adverb.

1 Betty thinks her sister's *very / completely* amazing at basketball.
2 When Australians go to Europe, they think everything is *extremely / really* ancient.
3 Last year in Egypt, I saw the pyramids and they were *very / absolutely* enormous.
4 That lady is *incredibly / absolutely* old – I think she's 102!
5 I hate it when people lie – I think it's *very / completely* bad.
6 Our sports teacher wanted us to run but it was *really / incredibly* freezing.
7 I go to bed early because I don't want to be *absolutely / completely* tired in the morning.
8 I love that painting – it's *absolutely / very* awesome.

## WRITING   An email

**1** Look at the advertisement about an activity holiday. Which sports will be available?

...................................................................
...................................................................

Try lots of new and different sports and activities at our

# HOLIDAY SPORTS WEEK

**Meet every day at 9.00 am in the Youth Hall.
Bring a friend and have lots of fun!**

Call Mick on 879630 for more information.

**2** Read the email below quickly. Which topics does Freddie cover?

idea for the holiday ☐
the sport he has chosen ☐
where the holiday centre is ☐
how you choose a sport ☐
how to book a place ☐
reasons for choosing the sport ☐

Send

Hi!
I saw this absolutely awesome idea for our holiday next week! It's an activity week. I phoned to get some more information. And guess what – we can decide which sports to do. How cool is that? They give us the chance to choose. You just have to say what you want to do and why.
I'm going to say rock-climbing. I think it is such a great sport and everyone can try it. You learn to be confident because if you are nervous, you might fall. You also have to trust your buddy – the one holding the rope. I think trying out new sports is lots of fun.
What sport would you choose and why?
See you soon,
Freddie

**3** Read the email again. These are Freddie's notes before he wrote the email. Number them 1–6 in the correct order.

| | |
|---|---|
| how we choose a sport | ☐ |
| idea for holiday | ☐ |
| skills you can learn | ☐ |
| my choice of sport | ☐ |
| why I chose it | ☐ |
| where I got information | ☐ |

**4** Now write an email to a friend of yours about the activity week.

- Make notes first about what to include.
- Write about 100 words.

# 4 From fire to snow

## VOCABULARY Extreme weather

**1** Write the words and phrases from the box under the picture.

| blow away | burn down | flood | flow | forecast | lightning | pour | power | rise | tornado |

a ........ tornado ........    d ..........................    g ..........................    i ..........................
b .......... rise ..........    e ..........................    h ..........................    j ..........................
c ..........................    f ...:......................

**2** Complete the sentences with the correct form of the words in exercise 1.

1 The .......................... for tomorrow is sunny with a chance of a shower.

2 Oh no! The .......................... has gone again – it always happens during storms. Where are the candles?

3 With all the forest fires at the moment, I think that many houses are going to .......................... .

4 I hate it when there's a .......................... – there's water everywhere.

5 The .......................... was like something out of a film – the wind was lifting everything up.

6 Oh look! That girl's hat is going to .......................... .

7 My grandfather loves watching the .......................... in the sky during a storm.

8 Have you got an umbrella? It's going to .......................... with rain later today.

9 The river is .......................... much faster than usual because of all the heavy rain.

10 Look at this line. It shows how high the river can .......................... when it rains a lot.

**3** Write the words from the box in the correct column.

| blow away | burn down | flood | flow |
| lightning | pour | rise | tornado |

| Water | Fire | Storm | Wind |
|-------|------|-------|------|
|       |      |       |      |

### EP Word profile *case*

Complete the sentences with the correct expression from the box.

| in case | in case of | in each case |
| in this case | new cases of |

1 My course is about how to rescue people .......................... an accident on the river.

2 I've packed some extra biscuits .......................... you get hungry.

3 There have been several .......................... upset stomachs recently.

4 These three phones have cameras and .......................... they take amazing photos.

5 All homework is usually due in on Mondays but .......................... it can be Tuesday.

In the picture weather panel:
Today 9°C
Tomorrow 24°C

# READING

**1** Read the article quickly. (Ignore the spaces.) Which text message do you think the girl in paragraph 3 sent her friend the next day?

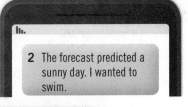

1 Wow! That was a crazy day yesterday!

2 The forecast predicted a sunny day. I wanted to swim.

3 Grandma and I found some amazing plants for sale.

**2** Look at these sentences from the text. What kind of word is missing?

> verb    adjective    pronoun    preposition

1 The mini tornado was a frightening event that started ........................... heavy rain …
2 The wind got ........................... , the sky went a strange colour …
3 … and the wind began to ........................... the roofs of the houses.
4 One girl, ........................... grandfather is the owner of a garden …

## EXAM TIPS

**Reading Part 5**
- Read the text through to get a good idea of what it is about.
- Look at the four options for each question and decide what type of word is tested – a verb, a noun, an adjective or something else?
- Read the text again and choose your answers.

**3** Read the text again and choose the correct word for each space.

## Kapiti mini tornado

At about 2 pm yesterday, high winds destroyed houses and trees **(0)** ....A.... bad weather hit the Kapiti coast in New Zealand.

The mini tornado was a frightening event that started **(1)** ........... heavy rain and a high wind. The wind got **(2)** ........... , the sky went a strange colour and huge balls of ice **(3)** ........... from the sky. This **(4)** ........... a lot of cars and buildings, and the wind began to **(5)** ........... the roofs off the houses.

One girl, **(6)** ........... grandfather is the owner of a shop selling things for the garden, was helping her grandmother to **(7)** ........... plants back inside the main building when it was hit by the tornado. Fortunately, she was not hurt, **(8)** ........... she was very scared by what happened.

The whole area was **(9)** ........... without power for a long time, and **(10)** ........... buildings needed repairs afterwards.

| | | | | | | | | |
|---|---|---|---|---|---|---|---|
| **0** | **A** | as | **B** | after | **C** | yet | **D** | unless |
| **1** | **A** | for | **B** | to | **C** | on | **D** | with |
| **2** | **A** | heavier | **B** | thicker | **C** | stronger | **D** | darker |
| **3** | **A** | pulled | **B** | broke | **C** | passed | **D** | fell |
| **4** | **A** | damaged | **B** | hurt | **C** | injured | **D** | lost |
| **5** | **A** | lift | **B** | flow | **C** | pick | **D** | rise |
| **6** | **A** | which | **B** | whose | **C** | that | **D** | who |
| **7** | **A** | turn | **B** | stay | **C** | move | **D** | keep |
| **8** | **A** | or | **B** | though | **C** | if | **D** | even |
| **9** | **A** | left | **B** | remained | **C** | held | **D** | dropped |
| **10** | **A** | plenty | **B** | many | **C** | lots | **D** | much |

# GRAMMAR  Past simple and *used to*

**1 Complete the sentences with the verbs in the past simple tense.**

1 Last week our maths teacher Mr Hutchins
.............................. (give) us extra homework.

2 He .............................. (not teach) us maths last year.

3 Nobody really knows why Jonathan
.............................. (fall off) his chair in class.

4 I .............................. (send) her a text about the party
yesterday.

5 Mum and I .............................. (meet) one of the new
teachers at the supermarket last week.

6 Angie and Frank .............................. (not tell) anyone
what they were doing.

7 The best film I .............................. (see) at the festival
was about a man and his dog.

8 This is where we .............................. (go) on holiday
last year.

**2 Complete the conversation with verbs from the box. Use the present simple or past simple form.**

| buy | do | help | know | not play |
|-----|----|----|----|----|
| not think | want | work | | |

**Mike:** What ¹ .............................. you ..............................
last weekend?

**Jack:** Nothing much. My grandparents
² .............................. a new computer.

**Mike:** Oh, ³ .............................. you ..............................
them to set it up?

**Jack:** Not really. Granddad ⁴ .............................. quite a
lot about computers.

**Mike:** That's right. He ⁵ .............................. in computers,
didn't he?

**Jack:** Yes, he did. He ⁶ .............................. a more
powerful computer to surf and play games on.

**Mike:** Wow! My grandparents ⁷ ..............................
computer games. I ⁸ .............................. they're
interested.

**Jack:** Well, mine are! They aren't old-fashioned at all.

**3 Write questions in the past simple tense for these answers.**

0 .....What time did you get up this morning?.....
I got up at about 7.30.

1 ..............................................................................
Yes, I did. I had some toast and jam.

2 ..............................................................................
I came to school by car this morning – Dad brought
me.

3 ..............................................................................
Yes, but I was nearly late because the roads were
very busy.

4 ..............................................................................
He didn't park at the school – I jumped out and
ran in!

**4 Write the words in the correct order to make sentences.**

1 to / live / used / Adrian / Canada / in
..............................................................................

2 to / He / used / a pair of / have / snowboots
..............................................................................

3 walk / to / He / didn't / school / to / used
..............................................................................

4 in his classes / used / French / speak / to / He
..............................................................................

5 to / He / go / used / on holiday / to / the lakes
..............................................................................

6 go / to / used / skiing / He
..............................................................................

7 to / used / a lot of / wear / He / clothes / warm
..............................................................................

8 dream / to / the snow! / He / use / about / didn't
..............................................................................

**5 What did Andreas used to do when he was a young boy? Write sentences.**

1 do boxing ✔
..............................................................................

2 eat green vegetables ✗
..............................................................................

3 play with a toy train set ✔
..............................................................................

4 climb trees ✔
..............................................................................

5 speak English ✗
..............................................................................

6 go to bed early ✔
..............................................................................

7 have lots of homework ✗
..............................................................................

8 play computer games ✗
..............................................................................

**6 ⊙ Correct the mistakes in these sentences or put a tick (✔) by any you think are correct.**

1 I meet her when I was nine years old at school.
..............................................

2 I go to the restaurant last Saturday with my friend.
..............................................

3 It was hard work but it was worth it.
..............................................

4 We use to study together and she use to hit me all
the time! ..............................................

5 We used to went biking together, but now we only
talk to each other on the phone. ..............................................

6 We weren't classmates, but we were used to talk a
lot after lessons. ..............................................

# VOCABULARY Phrasal verbs

**1 Choose the correct answer.**

There used to be a great restaurant just outside our village, but it had real problems recently. First, there was a huge storm and the wind blew all the outside tables and chairs [1] *away / up*. The rain was awful, but then the sun came [2] *down / out* and everywhere became very dry. This led to forest fires, and there was a fire at the restaurant so it completely burnt [3] *away / down.* The firefighters didn't arrive in time to put it [4] *away / out,* which was a shame because we all used to enjoy hanging [5] *out / down* there. It was after the fire that Tracey and Daniel split [6] *up / away.*

**2 Complete the sentences with the correct form of the phrasal verbs in the box.**

> blow away    burn down    come out
> hang out    put out    split up

1 My friends and I love ............................. at the mall on Saturday afternoons.
2 Many houses ............................. during the recent forest fires.
3 It's too windy to work outside – all the papers will ............................. .
4 Have you heard the news? Mitch and Filipa have ............................. .
5 Jonas helped the fire brigade ............................. the fire.
6 As we walked home, the sun ............................. at last.

## LISTENING

**1 Where can you find out what to do in extreme weather situations?**

1 the internet ☐
2 books ☐
3 school ☐
4 ask people (who?) ☐ .............................
5 your own ideas ☐ .............................

**2 ▶3 You will hear an interview with a girl called Lacey Anderson, who has started a blog about what do to in extreme weather situations. Listen to the interviewer's questions and write the missing words.**

1 Why did you decide to ............................. about the ............................. ?
2 Right. So ............................. a blog?
3 So what ............................. is on your blog?
4 And isn't your ............................. weather centre helping you now?
5 What about your parents – when did they get ............................. ?
6 Have other people ............................. been helpful?

**3 ... the information below. How similar or ... t is what the interviewer says to the ... ons that you have to answer?**

... y is Lacey's blog about the weather?
... She wants to become a TV weather presenter.
... She likes sharing her photos of extreme events.
... She thinks it's important because of where she lives.

**2** Lacey decided to keep a blog because
**A** it links people to the telephone helpline.
**B** she finds it an enjoyable kind of activity.
**C** it's the best form of communication for teens.

**3** What is the main message on Lacey's blog?
**A** Leave a dangerous area immediately.
**B** Watch the TV for up-to-date information.
**C** Protect things in your home until help arrives.

**4** Lacey is pleased with the weather centre's help because
**A** they've given her information that she didn't have before.
**B** they've saved her a huge amount of time and effort.
**C** they've agreed to charge very little for their forecasts.

**5** Lacey's parents got involved in her blog when
**A** they both gave up their full-time jobs.
**B** she asked them to write an article on firefighters.
**C** they learnt about a situation which had a bad result.

**6** Who has given Lacey financial support for her blog?
**A** her school
**B** the local newspaper
**C** a shop in the area

## EXAM TIPS

**Listening Part 2**
• Read the questions and all three options before you listen.
• The questions follow the order of information in the recording and show you what information to listen for.
• Listen and choose the best option for each question.
• When you listen the second time, check that the other options are wrong.

**4 ▶3 Now listen to the interview and for each question, choose the correct answer, A, B or C.**

# 5 You made it!

## VOCABULARY  Verbs for making things

**1** Match the verbs to their meanings.

| | | | | |
|---|---|---|---|---|
| 1 create | ....... | 6 mend/fix | ....... |
| 2 customise | ....... | 7 rebuild | ....... |
| 3 design | ....... | 8 recycle | ....... |
| 4 decorate | ....... | 9 stick | ....... |
| 5 invent | ....... | 10 sew | ....... |

a make or repair clothes by joining cloth using a needle and thread

b repair something that is broken or not working properly

c change something to make it suitable for a particular person or purpose

d make something that has never existed before

e make

f draw or plan

g add attractive things to something

h join two things, usually with glue

i collect used paper, glass, plastic and other things and use them again

j build again

**2** Choose two correct answers for each sentence.

1 I'm going to ............................. a new type of pocket to go inside trousers!
   **a** design  **b** rebuild  **c** create

2 Oh, look – I've just broken my phone. I'd better take it back to the shop and see if they can ............................. it.
   **a** create  **b** mend  **c** fix

3 One of my friends always ............................. her school bags with pictures of her favourite actor.
   **a** sticks  **b** customises  **c** decorates

4 These little leather flowers are so pretty. I'm going to ............................. a couple of them onto my new jacket.
   **a** stick  **b** sew  **c** decorate

5 My dad's an architect and he's ............................. a completely new type of building.
   **a** created  **b** recycled  **c** invented

6 My bike's very old and broken now, but I won't throw it away; I'll ............................. it instead.
   **a** recycle  **b** rebuild  **c** customise

**3** Complete the sentences with the verbs in the correct form. There is one verb in each set that you do not need.

1 | customise | decorate | rebuild | sew | stick |

A: This bag is so boring. I'd like to ............................. it with something like red hearts.

B: Oh, why don't you put your name on it and ............................. it completely?

A: Good idea! No one else will have one like it! Shall I ............................. some letters on?

B: Why not get some cotton and ............................. them on?

2 | design | fix | recycle | sew | stick |

A: Your bike isn't working again – you're going to have to ............................. it.

B: Oh, not again. Look at it! I don't know who ............................. this type of bike, but it's no good.

A: It looks like this part was just ............................. on with glue here.

B: I know! Useless! I think I'm going to ............................. this bike and buy myself a new one.

3 | create | decorate | design | recycle | sew |

A: I think that we can use this material again, you know, ............................. it.

B: Yes, we can ............................. something completely new!

A: Like a dress and jacket – all together? And we'll ............................. the material together.

B: OK, I'll ............................. the pockets in the shape of flowers.

4 | design | fix | invent | rebuild | stick |

A: That building's beautiful – the wall is so clever. Who ............................. it?

B: No idea, but it looks like they are going to ............................. it.

A: No, they haven't finished it yet. The artist also ............................. a completely new technique for using broken plates on the wall.

B: Really? Well, I wouldn't want to ............................. all those broken pieces together!

## READING

**1** Look at the top and bottom of the article on page 21. What do you think it is going to be about?

.................................................................................................................

.................................................................................................................

**2** Read the magazine article quickly and check your ideas.

## EXAM TIPS

**Reading Part 3**
- Read the text quickly to get a general idea of what it is about.
- If you don't understand any words in the text, don't worry; just try to get the general idea.
- Read the sentences and then read the text again. There may be words in the sentences that help you to understand any words you don't know in the text.

**3** ⬤ Look at the sentences about an artist. Read the text to decide if each sentence is correct or incorrect. If it is correct, write A. If it is incorrect, write B.

1 Haroshi started skateboarding when he was a very young child. _B_

2 Haroshi kept all of his old skateboards because they were valuable. _A_

3 By collecting skateboards, he learnt that they are all made in the same way. _B_

4 An early work he made was something to wear. _B_

5 Haroshi started to make new objects by recycling material. _A_

6 All of his sculptures represent the world of skateboarding. _B_

7 Haroshi attended art school in London. _A_

8 The sculpture *Ordinary Life* shows something that could happen to anyone. _A_

9 The artist Unkei used to put something inside his sculptures. _B_

10 The magazine *Teen Attack* recommends the exhibition. _B_

---

**EP** **Word profile** *look*

Complete the sentences with a form of *look* or a phrase using *look*.

1 I can't find my phone – I've _looked_ it everywhere.

2 That _look_ nice on you – blue matches your eyes!

3 I'm really _looking_ to the weekend – we're going to the beach.

4 Did you try the food at the party? It _looks_ delicious and tasted even better!

5 I told the police that the man _looks_ an old person.

6 It _look_ everyone is coming to your party!

---

# TeenAttack!

**Artist Focus: Haroshi**

*Every month we look at a different artist. We think Haroshi is super cool – he makes sculptures from skateboards. Read on.*

Haroshi is in his late 30s. He's a skateboarder but he also makes things from wood. He began skateboarding when he was 15 years old and he loved it. He used to skate every day. Now, if you know anything about skateboarding, you'll know that skateboards don't last forever because they break. But Haroshi didn't throw his out because he was fond of them. Over time he built up a big collection and at the same time he learnt about all the different types of skateboard. Surprisingly, not all skateboards are the same shape and actually they are often built in different ways. By the time he was 25 he had an enormous collection of old skateboards.

He decided he had to do something with them so he started to cut them up. As he was doing that, he noticed some interesting patterns in the wood. He then cut more and stuck them on top of each other. The first thing he created from the wood was a piece of jewellery. He created something new from something old.

Nowadays, however, he is known for his extremely large 3D wooden sculptures. His ideas generally come from skateboarding culture, ranging from skateboarding cats to cool trainers, but also everyday topics such as hurting yourself, getting better, being crazy about something and of course, growing up. All skateboarders will understand these. Haroshi has made over 40 pieces and each piece takes a very long time. There is no doubt that he is very talented but he's had no formal art training. He taught himself.

Haroshi held an exhibition in London last month and three of us from @teenattack went along. As we entered the first room we saw a huge bird that covered one wall. It was absolutely enormous! There was also a sculpture called *Ordinary life*. It looked like a broken leg – a very common problem, of course. It's incredible to think that these sculptures are all made from broken skateboards. But there's something else that is really interesting about Haroshi's work. In the twelfth century a Japanese sculptor called Unkei placed a glass ball in each of his works, to show the heart of the piece. Haroshi also places something inside his sculptures – a piece of broken skateboard. In this way, he gives his sculptures life. We think that is just awesome! Go and see the work for yourself!

*Next Month: Shona Wilson – an Australian artist who makes art from natural and plastic rubbish.*

## GRAMMAR  Past simple and continuous

**1  Choose the correct form of the verb.**

As I ¹ *was cycling / cycled* home from school
yesterday, I ² *was singing / sang* to myself because
I ³ *wasn't having / didn't have* any homework.
Suddenly, a family of ducks ⁴ *was walking / walked*
out into the road in front of me. Although I ⁵ *was
going / went* downhill quite fast I ⁶ *was managing /
managed* to get out of their way in time and I ⁷ *wasn't
hitting / didn't hit* any of them.

**2  Complete the sentences with the verbs in the past
continuous or past simple.**

1  When I was young, I ............................ (want) to be
a pilot.
2  Maggie ............................ (text) a friend when her
mother ............................ (call) her for dinner.
3  What ............................ (do) last night?
I ............................ (watch) TV with my family.
4  Rick ............................ (take) my photo and
............................ (upload) it to Facebook.
5  No one ............................ (know) what to do for the
homework project.
6  I last ............................ (see) my cousin when she
............................ (visit) us two years ago.
7  Monique ............................ (walk) home from school
when her mum ............................ (drive) past her.
8  Jules ............................ (win) the competition and
we ............................ (hear) the news last night.

**3  Complete the text with the verbs in the box in the
correct form. There is one negative verb.**

> add    be    can    chat    decide    get
> keep    look    put    receive    send    want

Yesterday my friends and I ¹ ............................ during
the morning break when Jake ² ............................
a text from our friend Aysha. She was sick and she
³ ............................ come to school for the rest of
the week. So we ⁴ ............................ to send her
something. We ⁵ ............................ to send her a photo
of her friends with a message along the bottom that
said 'Get well soon' but, unfortunately, the younger
students ⁶ ............................ jumping up and down in
the picture. It ⁷ ............................ funny but annoying!
Finally, we ⁸ ............................ a good picture.
We ⁹ ............................ it into a special program on
the computer and ¹⁰ ............................ our text and
our names. It ¹¹ ............................ really good! While
I ¹² ............................ it, the bell rang. Perfect timing!

**4  Read the conversation and complete the
questions below.**

**Sam:**  What did you do in art last week?
**Toby:**  We talked about our end-of-year project.
**Sam:**  But what happened? I heard there was a
problem.
**Toby:**  Well, yes. The teacher left the room for a
minute. While we were talking, Sarah was
finishing her drawing of butterflies, and as
she was mixing her paints, suddenly there
was a loud noise – I think it was thunder. It
made us all jump but Sarah spilled her paint
everywhere. We were all laughing when the
teacher came back into the room.
**Sam:**  Uh oh! Not good!
**Toby:**  Well, it was OK because we explained, but
I don't think Sarah is doing butterflies for her
end-of-year project any more!

0  What .... *did the students talk about in art*
.... *last week* ............................ ?
The end-of-year project.
1  What ............................................................ ?
Finishing her drawing of butterflies.
2  What ............................................................ ?
A loud noise.
3  What ............................................................ ?
She spilled her paints.
4  Who ............................................................ ?
The teacher.
5  Why ............................................................ ?
Because they explained to her.

**5  ⊙  Correct the mistakes in these sentences or
put a tick (✔) by any you think are correct.**

1  Last year, I go to a place in Mexico named *Mazatlán*.
............................
2  I met him at school. I talk to my other friend, and he
came to meet me. ............................
3  Last weekend was fantastic and I had a lot of fun.
............................
4  We were dancing all night! ............................
5  When we met our friends in the park they
played football. ............................

## VOCABULARY   Time adverbs

**1  Choose the correct adverb.**

What a day it was when we had our maths test!
¹ *First / Later*, we walked into the classroom and
² *suddenly / then* we sat down. ³ *First / Next*,
we got out our books. ⁴ *Suddenly / Finally*,
there was a huge bang and everyone jumped.
Our teacher discovered that it was just a noise
from the factory across the street. ⁵ *Finally /
Next*, the teacher gave us our test papers and
we began. ⁶ *Later / First*, we discovered that a
fire had started in the factory – it nearly burnt
down! That was the day I got 100% in maths!

**2  Complete the email with the adverbs in
the box.**

> Finally    First    later
> Next    Suddenly    then

---

**Send**

Hi Alan,
You didn't miss a lot in art today.
¹ ............................. , we had to choose
what we wanted to paint. Mr Jenkins
had brought some fruit in and we had
to choose one piece. I know – it was so
boring. ² ............................. , he asked us to
choose either pencil or black pen to draw
it, and ³ ............................. we went up to
his desk to get the paper and start our
work. ⁴ ............................. , the fire alarm
rang! We all had to go and stand in the
playground, and we were there for a long
time. ⁵ ............................. , we went back
into the art class, but there were only five
minutes of the lesson left, so Mr Jenkins
said to finish the work ⁶ ............................. .
Hope you get better soon,
Stevie

---

## WRITING   A short text

See Prepare to write box, Student's Book page 13.

**1  Read these two questions and then read the email
below. Which question does it answer – A or B?
Does the writer include everything from the question?**

....................................................................................

**A**
I want to find a suitable present for my
younger sister. Can you give me an idea
of what to buy? You know my sister – why
would she like it? And where can I buy it?
Thanks,
Jo

**B**
Can you tell me about the present you made
recently, and if it was a good idea? Please
describe what you made and tell me who it
was for. Also, did the person like it?
Thanks,
Jo

Hi Jo,
It was Mum's birthday last week and I wanted
to make her something. I made a bag, which I
decorated with some beautiful flowers made from
buttons. When I gave her the present, she told me
she loved it!
See you soon,
Maxine

**2  Do these sentences come from an answer to question
A or question B?**

1  It was a photo of me and I decorated it with
   red hearts.                                     .......
2  I think it would be nice because she likes
   playing games.                                  .......
3  The toy shop in town next to the post office
   sells them.                                     .......
4  It was her birthday last week.                  .......
5  She said it was really pretty.                  .......
6  What about a book of games?                     .......

**3  Read Maxine's email again. Do these ideas come from
the beginning, the middle or the end of the email?**

1  her mother's opinion            ...........................
2  how she made the present        ...........................
3  who the present was for         ...........................

**4  Write your own short answer to question A. Write about
45–50 words.**

- Use three main sentences – a beginning, a middle and
  an end.
- Make sure you answer the question fully.
- Check your spelling and grammar.

## VOCABULARY   Health

**1 Complete the word puzzle, using the clues on the right.**

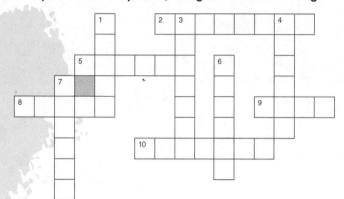

**Across**

2 say that something is wrong
5 make something less
8 stay away from someone or something
9 cover or surround something with material, for example
10 stop something from happening

**Down**

1 lose blood
3 treat an illness or injury by cutting someone's body
4 hurt a person, animal or part of your body
6 have an illness or other health problem
7 do what someone or something says you should do

**2 Write the letters in the correct order to make words and complete the sentences.**

1 P O A T E E R
   The doctors are going to ............................. on Mikael at eight o'clock.

2 D E C U E R
   If you have a fever, you can try to ............................. it by putting something cold on your head.

3 E B D E L
   Anna hit her nose and it started to ............................. .

4 D A V I O
   If you go to Australia, you should ............................. the sun – it's really hot!

5 L O L W O F
   If you ............................. a diet, you should also exercise.

6 G O C P L I M N I A N
   Jason is ............................. about his cold again.

7 V E P T E R N
   Drinking lots of orange juice can help you to ............................. a cold.

8 J U I N E R D
   The footballer has ............................. himself again and can't play.

9 P R A W
   Take the bandage and ............................. it twice around your ankle.

10 F U S E R S F
   Joshua ............................. from allergies in spring.

**3 Complete the article with the correct form of the verbs in the box.**

avoid   bleed   complain   follow   injure
operate   prevent   reduce   suffer   wrap

# TAKING CARE OF ... YOUR HEAD

This week we look at our head. One very common thing that many of you [1] ............................. about is headaches, especially when you're using the computer. You can [2] ............................. these problems with headaches by [3] ............................. the amount of time you spend looking at a screen.

Some of you play a lot of sports and occasionally [4] ............................. yourselves. Tom, from the UK, had a very bad accident while skiing, and his doctor had to [5] ............................. on his head in hospital. Now Tom has to [6] ............................. a bandage around it every day for a few weeks. Poor Tom!

Astrid in Holland [7] ............................. from migraines, that is, very bad headaches, and she has to [8] ............................. the instructions on her medicine bottle very carefully. She says she can sometimes [9] ............................. a very bad migraine by drinking lots of water and also getting outside and breathing fresh air. Thanks for that tip, Astrid!

That's it on all those head things! Next week we look at the nose: we received an email from Jon in Sweden. He noticed that his friend's nose was [10] ............................. and he didn't know what to do. What do you think? If you know the answer, you could win a prize. Send your answers in to: arabellasilkie@yourmagazine.com

# READING

**1** Read about two strange medical problems and choose the correct title for each text.

   **1** Don't eat everything!      **2** This is for you, and you, and you …      **3** Heartbeat drink

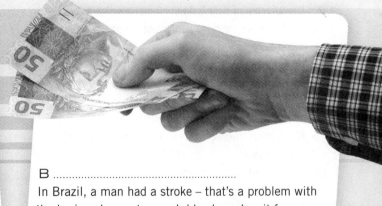

**A** ..................................................................

Have you ever wondered what would happen if you only drank fizzy drinks, like cola or lemonade? And you drank them for a very long time? Well, one woman in Monaco did just that, for 15 years. At one point she went to hospital because she didn't feel very well. The doctors did some tests and found that she had extremely low levels of the mineral potassium (K) in her blood, and her heart wasn't beating normally. The doctors asked her some questions and she said that there was no history of heart problems in her family. But she said that when she was 15, she started drinking about two litres of cola and other fizzy drinks every day, and she still did so. She didn't even drink water. She stopped drinking the fizzy drinks and a week later her blood and her heartbeat were back to normal. The doctors told her she mustn't drink any more fizzy drinks!

**B** ..................................................................

In Brazil, a man had a stroke – that's a problem with the brain, when not enough blood reaches it for a short time. The man suddenly became very generous: he gave away money and he bought sweets for children he met on the street. He had to leave his job in a large company where he used to deal with money. He couldn't even manage his own money any more and he started to give it away. The doctors who were looking after the man were interested because the change in his behaviour was different from the usual changes after a stroke. They did several tests on his brain and found which parts of the brain didn't have enough blood in them, which helped to explain his behaviour. They gave him a type of medicine to help him, and two years later, he feels much better, but has decided not to go back to work as he still can't manage money and is too generous. Fortunately, his wife can look after him and his money!

**2** Read the texts again and write A, B or both A and B.

Who …

   **1** had a family history that interested the doctors? .......
   **2** had a family member to take care of them? .......
   **3** suffered from a limited diet? .......
   **4** had a problem that involved their blood in some way? .......
   **5** has to live with the condition because it cannot be changed? .......
   **6** surprised people with their behaviour? .......
   **7** got better very quickly? .......
   **8** lost money because of the problem? .......

**3** Match the highlighted words in the texts to the meanings.

   **1** happening because of good luck ...........................
   **2** giving lots of something, e.g. time or money ...........................
   **3** be in control of something ...........................
   **4** usually ...........................
   **5** wanted to know something ...........................

**EP Word profile** *only*

Rewrite the following sentences, using *only*.

   **1** We have two very short exercises for homework today.
      We have .................................................................. .

   **2** We arrived yesterday. We haven't been here long.
      We've .................................................................. .

   **3** A stomach ache? I don't think your condition is very serious.
      You .................................................................. .

   **4** You have to be online to do the homework.
      You can ..................................................................
      .................................................................. .

   **5** My friend has a really annoying habit of talking very loudly.
      If ..................................................................
      .................................................................. .

   **6** My sister is six so she's too young to understand.
      She can't ..................................................................
      .................................................................. .

# GRAMMAR  Modals (1): Obligation and necessity

## 1  Choose the correct modal verb.

1 Doctors say that we *ought to* / *shouldn't* eat five pieces of fruit a day.

2 If your nose starts bleeding, you *should* / *must* hold your head forward.

3 If you don't feel well, you *don't have to* / *must* go to school.

4 If you are really sick, you *don't have to* / *shouldn't* do physical exercise.

5 Most of us *should* / *doesn't have to* drink more water.

6 You *must* / *ought to* wear your school uniform to school.

7 Your leg is bleeding badly. We *ought to* / *shouldn't* see a doctor.

8 You *don't have to* / *mustn't* bring your own lunch – it's provided.

## 2  Write the words in the correct order to make sentences.

1 do / has / dinner / to / Jackie / the washing up / after

.......................................................................
.......................................................................

2 leave / his homework / until / dinner / mustn't / after / Louis

.......................................................................
.......................................................................

3 the nurse / ought / his arm / Frank / to / to / show

.......................................................................
.......................................................................

4 The boys / go / to / mustn't / school / sick / they / because / are

.......................................................................
.......................................................................

5 go / You / in the rain / shouldn't / an umbrella / out / without

.......................................................................
.......................................................................

6 doesn't / lay / have / the table / Lucinda / to

.......................................................................
.......................................................................

7 have / the dishwasher / William / put / to / the dishes / in / doesn't

.......................................................................
.......................................................................

8 ought / to / stop / on / her computer / playing / Rachel

.......................................................................
.......................................................................

## 3  Complete the text with the modal verbs in the box.

| don't have to   have to   mustn't   ought to   shouldn't |

This month it's smoothies! A smoothie is fruit with yoghurt or milk. Yum! First, you
¹ ............................... get a blender – that's an item of electrical equipment. Your mum or dad should have one. Put some yoghurt in the blender and then add the fruit.
You ² ............................... spend a lot of money – but you ³ ............................... try to get fresh fruit. When you've put the fruit and yoghurt into the blender, you mix it and that's it – easy! It ⁴ ............................... take more than two or three minutes! One thing – you ⁵ ............................... let very young children use the blender because it can be dangerous.

## 4  Complete the sentences with a suitable modal verb and a verb from the box.

| finish   help   listen   play   think |

**A:** Hey, Anna, I can't do this homework. It's really hard.

**B:** You ¹ ............................... in class. Then the homework would be easy!

**A:** I know, but I don't understand what the teacher is saying.

**B:** Sure, but you ² ............................... with your phone in class.

**A:** But history is so boring.

**B:** You ³ ............................... that everything you do at school is boring.

**A:** But it is! Why are we doing this?

**B:** Well, we ⁴ ............................... school before we can go to college or work.

**A:** I guess. But will you still help me with my homework? Please?

**B:** I ⁵ ............................... you but I will because you're my sister!

## 5  ⊙  Choose the correct sentence in each pair.

1 a You mustn't forget to bring your picnic bag.
  b You mustn't forget to bring your picnic bag.

2 a I wanted to go to the beach but my friend said that we should not.
  b I wanted to go to the beach but my friend said that we do not.

3 a I don't know what I ought to do because I think my friend is a bad person.
  b I don't know what I have to do because I think my friend is a bad person.

## VOCABULARY  Pronouns with *some, any, every* and *no*

**1** Complete the sentences with *thing, where* or *one*.

1 There's some............ at the door – who do you think it is?
2 I've looked every............ and I can't find the book.
3 I want to get some............ special for your birthday.
4 She went to the party but she didn't know any............ there.
5 If every............ helps, it'll be much quicker and easier.
6 I have some............ exciting to tell you. Let's meet later today.
7 No ............ spoke to me all day. It was very quiet.
8 I'm sure your bag is some............ in the house. Have you looked in your room?

**2** Complete the sentences with the words in the box.

> anyone    anything    everyone    everything
> nothing    no one    something

1 This is ............................. you need when you send a letter.
2 There isn't ............................. to do while you wait, so take a book with you.
3 Have you got ............................. you need to make a pizza?
4 I don't want to go to a different school because I won't know ............................. there.
5 There's ............................. left to eat – we have to wait until Mum gets home with the shopping.
6 ............................. in my class loves the biology teacher – she's so funny!
7 ............................. did the homework and the teacher was very angry!

## LISTENING

**1** Tick the apps you have on your phone/computer.

games ☐
maps ☐
social media ☐
photography ☐
school ☐
time organisation ☐
other ☐
(What? .........................)

**2** ▶4 You will hear a podcast in which the presenter is talking about apps for teens. Listen and tick what the apps do.

tells you the number of hours you slept ☐
tells you how healthy your food is ☐
tells you how far you have run ☐
gives you prizes and rewards ☐
tells you what kind of exercise to do ☐
plays your favourite music ☐

### EXAM TIPS

**Listening Part 3**
• Try to predict what information might fit in the spaces.
• You will only need to write one or two words, or a number.
• Write any numbers in figures not words.

**3** Read the notes about the podcast and write down what kind of information (name, number, etc.) you might need in each space.

1 ........................... 4 ...........................
2 ........................... 5 ...........................
3 ........................... 6 ...........................

---

**NOTES ON APPS FOR CARLA**

**App 1**

Name of app: **(1)** ...........................

Price of app: **(2)** € ...........................

**App 2**

Minimum number of days to keep avatar alive:
**(3)** ...........................

Game gives advice on **(4)** ...........................

**App 3**

Developed by a **(5)** ...........................

This year's competition prize: **(6)** ...........................

---

**4** Now look at the type of information for each space and choose the correct answer.

1 girl's name / app title
2 a number / a date
3 a phrase like *for a long time* / a number
4 a noun / an adjective
5 name of a person / a job
6 an object / a person

**5** ▶4 ● Listen again and fill in the missing information in the numbered spaces.

# 7 Sound checks

## VOCABULARY   Music

**1** Match the words to their meanings.

| | | | | |
|---|---|---|---|---|
| 1 | concert hall | ....... | **a** | a person who plays songs on the radio or at events |
| 2 | DJ | ....... | **b** | a short recording that you can see on a website |
| 3 | celebrity | ....... | **c** | a person who plays music, especially as part of their job |
| 4 | musician | ....... | **d** | when someone controls how the music is made in a studio |
| 5 | guitarist | ....... | **e** | a TV station that shows mainly music |
| 6 | studio | ....... | **f** | a room where recordings are made |
| 7 | festival | ....... | **g** | a person who plays the guitar |
| 8 | live | ....... | **h** | seen or heard as it happens |
| 9 | music channel | ....... | **i** | a building where you can listen to music |
| 10 | sound technician | ....... | **j** | a person who is famous, especially in entertainment |
| 11 | production | ....... | **k** | a series of special events over several days, usually entertainment |
| 12 | video clip | ....... | **l** | a person who checks the quality of sound |

**2** Choose the correct answer.

1 We sat up all night and watched *video clips / concert halls*.
2 I think that seeing *music channel / live music* is the best thing in the world.
3 Do you want to come to 'Jazz in the Grass'? It's a *studio / festival* starting next week.
4 Have you heard the *guitarist / sound technician* on that song?
5 My grandparents never watch *music channels / sound technicians*.
6 I love listening to Pete Frank's choices in the morning – he's such a good *musician / DJ*.
7 There's a beautiful old *concert hall / production* in the city centre.
8 To be a *guitarist / sound technician*, you have to understand how sound works.

**3** Complete the text with the words in the box.

> celebrities   DJ   festivals   guitarist   musician   production   sound technician   studio

### Jobs in the music industry

Many young people love music and want to work in music when they leave school. Would you like to be the ¹ ............................. that everyone listens to in the morning? You can play your favourite music for a job! Or perhaps you've learnt to play the guitar at school and have become an excellent ² ............................. . Of course, the people in these jobs are often very famous – they're ³ ............................. . But what about the other jobs in the industry? There is the ⁴ ............................. , who has to check hundreds of things in music recordings. Or you could work in ⁵ ............................. and you might have to rent a ⁶ ............................. . And, of course, somebody has to find ⁷ ............................. for the artists to play at. There are a huge number of jobs available in the music industry and you don't have to be a ⁸ ............................. to get in.

**4** Complete the dialogue with words from exercise 1.

**A:** You know the band Gogo? Which ¹ ............................. do you admire most?
**B:** I really like Joe Bing, the new ² ............................. . He plays the guitar so well!
**A:** I agree! Did you see the new ³ ............................. on the internet last night? Amazing!
**B:** Yes. It was also on TV on the ⁴ ............................. .
**A:** And did you see that the band is going to be at the music ⁵ ............................. in town in the summer? Really exciting!
**B:** I know! And they're playing inside at the town ⁶ ............................. just before the festival – and Josh and I have tickets!
**A:** Oh, you don't! I'm so jealous!

# READING

**1** Read the text and tick (✔) the ideas that are mentioned.

1 why some people think recording studios are important ☐
2 why some studios have closed down ☐
3 how to use your bedroom as a studio ☐
4 how studios have changed ☐

**2** Read what Anais and Allan say about recording studios. Which sentence is correct?

1 Anais and Allan have the same opinion.
2 Anais and Allan make good points but they disagree.
3 Anais and Allan agree on some points but not all.

**3** Read the rest of the text and think of what kind of word fits each space, e.g. noun, verb, preposition.

0 ........*adverb*........

| | |
|---|---|
| 1 .............................. | 6 .............................. |
| 2 .............................. | 7 .............................. |
| 3 .............................. | 8 .............................. |
| 4 .............................. | 9 .............................. |
| 5 .............................. | 10 .............................. |

## EXAM TIPS

**Reading Part 5**
- Read the text through to get a good idea of what it is about.
- Read the text again and choose your answers.
- Check the other three options to make sure they don't fit.

**4** 🔘 Now read the text again and choose the correct word for each space.

| 0 | **A** around | **B** through | **C** inside | **D** beyond |
|---|---|---|---|---|
| 1 | **A** between | **B** during | **C** from | **D** since |
| 2 | **A** gained | **B** meant | **C** allowed | **D** let |
| 3 | **A** earns | **B** spends | **C** charges | **D** costs |
| 4 | **A** lot | **B** plenty | **C** many | **D** several |
| 5 | **A** moments | **B** opportunities | **C** periods | **D** occasions |
| 6 | **A** can | **B** need | **C** ought | **D** have |
| 7 | **A** sticking | **B** giving | **C** creating | **D** aiming |
| 8 | **A** Although | **B** If | **C** Or | **D** Unless |
| 9 | **A** turn | **B** get | **C** make | **D** set |
| 10 | **A** remain | **B** wait | **C** leave | **D** happen |

## How important are recording studios today?

I think they are really important. Musicians have to have somewhere to record and the quality of the sound is so much better. Imagine your favourite band recording in their living room! It wouldn't be the same.
*Anais, aged 15*

Only old people have heard of them! Nowadays, with a good laptop and the right software, anyone can record and put their music on the internet! Easy!
*Allan, aged 15*

## RECORDING STUDIOS

Recording studios have been **(0)** ....A.... for a long time. However, they have changed greatly **(1)** ........... the last 50 years and especially recently, as digital technology has **(2)** ........... more people to record music in their own homes. Nowadays, it **(3)** ........... very little to develop good recordings and upload them to the internet, and a **(4)** ........... of the larger studios have closed down because of this.
At the same time, there are new **(5)** ........... for individuals wanting to start small studios. These people **(6)** ........... offer a wide range of services apart from music, such as recording novels and **(7)** ........... unusual sound effects. **(8)** ........... they have the money, some musicians prefer to **(9)** ........... up their own recording studio. Then they are able to **(10)** ........... independent of record companies and record their music exactly how they want.

## EP Word profile *just*

Write *just* in the correct place.

1 We had a lovely holiday last year – it ........... was ........... wonderful!
2 Jonathan got ........... the bus ........... in time.
3 This song ........... is ........... what I wanted.
4 I've ........... about ........... finished my homework.
5 The ........... test isn't ........... about grammar.
6 I'm nearly ready. I'll be there in ........... a ........... minute.
7 Have you heard the news about Teri? It ........... is ........... awful!
8 I've ........... got my ........... results. I'm so excited!

## GRAMMAR  Present perfect and past simple

**1** Choose the correct answer.

1 I first *heard / have heard* this song years ago.
2 My favourite band *has played / played* in this town before.
3 There *were / have been* huge crowds last time they were here.
4 Mandy *hasn't listened / didn't listen* to that song last night.
5 Ana can't go to the ballet and so she *offered / has offered* her ticket to her friend.
6 *Have you ever played / did you ever play* the violin before?
7 Our music teacher *has recorded / recorded* a song with his band last week.
8 Denis and his friend *performed / have performed* live at their end-of-year concert last week.

**2** Read the sentences and put *already*, *just* or *yet* in the right place.

                          *already*

0 Don't put your shoes on the table. I've told you that hundreds of times.

1 Jasmine has bought a new laptop. It's still in the box.

2 I haven't done my homework.

3 I don't want to see that film – I've seen it. Jules and I went last week.

4 Most of our class haven't made their choices for next year.

5 Miguel's phoned. He's missed the bus. He'll be here later.

6 Mum and Dad have seen me perform many times.

7 We haven't chosen our school play.

8 I've heard the most amazing song! Let's find it online.

**3** Complete the text with the verb in the simple past or present perfect. Put the adverb in the correct position where necessary.

I ¹ ........................... (take part in/just) an amazing arts project, which actually ² ........................... (begin) by accident. Perhaps you ³ ........................... (hear) of the Virtual Choir? A choir is a group of people who sing together. It all ⁴ ........................... (start) when the musician Eric Whitacre, who ⁵ ........................... (write) a lot of music, including songs, watched a video clip of a girl singing his music. It ⁶ ........................... (give) Eric the idea for the virtual choir. I got this message from a friend: 'I ⁷ ........................... (see/just) this amazing thing. This guy ⁸ ........................... (invite) people to record their voice and upload it to a site. I ⁹ ........................... (do/already) mine. Do yours now, then we can be in the same choir.' Nothing unusual about that except that my friend and I live on different sides of the world! And that is how the virtual choir ¹⁰ ........................... (happen). What a great experience for these two friends living so far apart!

**4** Correct the mistakes in these sentences or put a tick (✔) by any you think are correct.

1 I have just buy a computer game. ...........................
2 I have just received your letter. ...........................
3 We met at school and since then we are friends.
   ...........................
4 Well, I've met my friends at school seven years ago. ...........................
5 I know Claudia since I was a child. ...........................

## VOCABULARY  Word families

Write the correct form of the word in brackets to complete the sentence.

1 The school band made a ........................... of a famous song for the school website. (record)
2 The last time I saw a live ........................... was in the summer holidays. (perform)
3 I saw a really funny ........................... on TV last night. (advertise)
4 Jason is such a ........................... person – he can play three instruments. (music)
5 Our teacher ........................... the winners of the competition. (announcement)
6 My greatest ........................... this year is passing my ballet exam. (achieve)

## WRITING An informal letter

See Prepare to write box, Student's Book page 45.

**1** Read this advertisement for a music festival and read Maria's letter. What did she enjoy most at the festival?

### MUSIC FESTIVAL IN THE BLACK MOUNTAINS

3 days of amazing music from all over the world

**Featuring:**
Vania from Argentina
The Boys from Estonia
and many more!

Email us for more information –
blackmountainsmusicfestival@blackmountains.com

---

Dear Jake,

<u>I have just returned</u> from an awesome school trip. We got back a couple of days ago and <u>I would like</u> to tell you about it!
We attended the Black Mountains Music Festival, which is held in the Black Mountains in late August. We went with our music class and our super music teacher, Ms Jones. <u>She is</u> so cool. The festival takes place every year and it lasts for three days. Musicians come from all over the world, so we heard a lot of different styles. I particularly enjoyed a group from New Zealand – their guitarist was just amazing! Now <u>I am going</u> to learn how to play the guitar!
Have you ever been to a music festival? Tell me all about it!

Love,

Maria

---

## EXAM TIPS

**Writing Part 3 (an informal letter)**
- When you write an informal letter, remember to use suitable phrases to start and end your letter.
- You are writing to a friend, so use short forms and informal words and phrases.

**2** Read the letter again. Answer the questions.

1 What phrases to start and end the letter does Maria use?

......................... ..............................

2 Find four informal words or phrases.

......................... ..............................

......................... ..............................

3 Write the underlined phrases as short forms.

......................... ..............................

......................... ..............................

**3** Rewrite the sentences with the correct time phrase in the box.

> every couple of days    every year    fortnight    weekly

1 We have to do maths homework every Friday at our school.
We have to do ............................................. .
2 We have an annual holiday at the seaside.
We go ............................................. .
3 At our last school, there were team baseball matches every two weeks.
At our last school, we had ........................................ .
4 Susie and I play tennis two or three times a week.
Susie and I ............................................. .

**4** Read this task and complete the table with notes for your answer.

> For my homework project, I have to write about a music festival in a different country. Tell me about a music festival in your country and what information I should include.

| Where is it? | |
|---|---|
| When is it? | |
| How long is it? | |
| What type of music is it? | |
| What do you like most about it? | |

**5** ⬤ Write your letter in about 100 words.

- Think of informal words and phrases you can use.
- Remember to use short forms.
- Use a suitable phrase to start and end your letter.
- Remember to check your spelling and grammar.

## VOCABULARY Describing buildings

**1** **Find adjectives in the word square (→ ↓ ↗ ↘) below to match the meanings.**

1 happening or starting a short time ago ...........................
2 new or different to what was there before ...........................
3 special and interesting ...........................
4 comfortable and warm ...........................
5 done in a certain style for a long time ...........................
6 relating to the present time, not the past ...........................
7 important or likely to be important in history ...........................
8 completely new ...........................
9 popular for a long time, and of good quality ...........................
10 extremely good, exciting or surprising ...........................
11 the earliest form of something ...........................

| S | P | E | C | T | A | C | U | L | A | R | N |
|---|---|---|---|---|---|---|---|---|---|---|---|
| O | R | P | K | P | Q | Z | N | L | N | F | L |
| R | G | E | C | L | A | S | S | I | C | A | M |
| I | F | G | C | B | G | V | Q | L | N | M | W |
| G | M | O | D | E | R | N | X | O | C | E | U |
| I | R | F | R | D | N | D | I | I | N | N | N |
| N | P | J | L | Q | C | T | R | D | B | K | U |
| A | M | C | Z | T | I | O | N | P | F | R | S |
| L | F | R | K | D | T | A | S | J | R | W | U |
| J | C | R | A | S | R | H | M | Y | E | J | A |
| M | M | R | I | B | V | F | B | W | S | R | L |
| J | T | H | M | M | Y | M | L | L | H | L | T |

**2** **Choose the correct adjective.**

1 My bedroom is very small but *historic / cosy*.
2 Tom and Maggie's home is *unusual / recent* because it is a boat.
3 This room has *spectacular / historic* views over the mountains.
4 The new museum in town has three lifts on the outside. It's very *modern / brand new*.
5 I've never seen a kitchen like this before. It's very *recent / unusual*.
6 Be careful with my phone – I got it yesterday so it's *fresh / brand new*!
7 The mountain village is full of *traditional / fresh* stone cottages.
8 The architect had a lot of *classic / fresh* ideas for the school library that the students will like.
9 When I visit a town I don't know, I always walk around and look at the *fresh / historic* buildings.
10 Have you noticed the *recent / traditional* trend of wearing shorts everywhere?

**3** **Complete the conversation with the words in the box.**

> cosy    modern    original    spectacular
> traditional    unusual

**Mum:** So, Rachel, how shall we decorate your bedroom?

**Rachel:** I don't want to keep the ¹ ........................... colour! It's horrible! Can I have blue, maybe a pale blue?

**Mum:** Yes, that's nice. Also, we can also make a feature of the ² ........................... view from the window, across to the mountains, you know, like we saw in that TV programme last night.

**Rachel:** That's a good idea. They painted the wall of the window a dark colour. It would be a bit different, you know, ³ ........................... .

**Mum:** OK. Do you want a ⁴ ........................... English style for the furniture, things made out of wood?

**Rachel:** I'm not sure. I'd like it to be ⁵ ........................... , you know, up to date!

**Mum:** Sure, well, we can buy some new things made out of wood. It's a small and ⁶ ........................... room and I think wood would look lovely.

**Rachel:** Cool, Mum! When can we go shopping?

## READING

**1** Look at the pictures. Read the texts quickly and match each text to a picture.

 1 .......  2 .......  3 .......

# What does your bedroom look like?

Nowadays there are so many ways to decorate your bedroom and so many programmes and magazines with ideas, so no excuses for boring rooms! We spoke to some teens who described their rooms to us.

**A**

My room is full of things – I've got quite a big make-up collection on a small table and then some shoes (I've got about five pairs of trainers) under the table. All over the room there are lots of unusual photos that I got from the internet, and then I put them into frames. I've also got souvenirs from holidays in the US. Everywhere I go, I always pick up interesting things to fill my room. I've always collected glass animals. My friends think it's unusual and the best animal I have is a yellow glass owl. The collection is on shelves on the wall. And I've got small lights around my mirror. I love the effect. All together it looks different.

*Astrid, aged 14, Canada*

**B**

My room is based on my favourite colour – red! Red for me is everything – it's my favourite colour, the colour of my football club and it's in the flag of the UK. So I have a red wall with photos of classic cars, which I love and my dad does too. In fact one of the pictures used to belong to him so it's lasted ages. Then I have my bed with a plain red cover and a couple of cushions on it. The desk area is white and I've got lots of boxes with all my things in. I don't like to have lots of things lying around. The best thing about my room is that my friends think it's awesome! I guess that's because it's at the top of the house and away from my parents.

*Yuri, aged 15, Russia*

**C**

This is my room and I really like it because it's my space. I have shelves full of books which I love but I also have a huge screen that I play Xbox on with my friends. The walls are bright green and the bed covers are black. I used to have a Star Wars-themed room but it was too black and I didn't like it. But when the lights are turned off at night, I can still see the stars on the ceiling. I really like that – it's spectacular. The desk area is usually covered with my schoolbooks and my laptop. In my opinion, it's more comfortable than any other room in the house.

*Franklin, aged 15, USA*

**2** Read the text again and write A, B or C.

Who …
1 is tidy? .......
2 has a big choice of shoes? .......
3 plays computer games? .......
4 likes the night sky? .......
5 collects things? .......
6 reads a lot? .......
7 has something that belonged to a family member? .......
8 is always looking for things for their room? .......

**3** What's your bedroom like? Complete the table.

| furniture | bed, |
|---|---|
| technology | |
| main colours in your room | |
| favourite objects | |
| what you can see from your window | |
| something you would like to change | |
| something you would never change | |
| adjectives to describe your room | |

### EP Word profile *last*

**Match the meanings of *last* to the example sentences.**

1 final ....... a The head's talk lasted for ages.
2 most recent ....... b Maggie got the last ticket for the film tonight.
3 most recently ....... c This is the last day to give in your homework.
4 continue ....... d I've started playing basketball since I saw you last.
5 remaining ....... e The last book I read was a horror story.

# GRAMMAR  Comparative and superlative adjectives

**1** Complete the table with comparative and superlative adjectives.

|  | Comparative | Superlative |
|---|---|---|
| fresh |  |  |
| big |  |  |
| brave |  |  |
| cosy |  |  |
| original |  |  |
| recent |  |  |

**2** Complete these sentences with the adjective in brackets and *as … as, less* or *the least*.

**1** In 2014 there was no building in the world which was ........................................................ the Burj Khalifa in Dubai. (tall)

**2** I chose ........................................................ chair in the lounge to sit on because I was the youngest. (comfortable)

**3** This programme is ........................................................ than last week's. (disappointing)

**4** That film was ........................................................ one of the series. (exciting)

**5** Filipa is ........................................................ Joana; they're both great girls to be with. (lively)

**6** Some people write about anything online. I found a blog about ........................................................ musical instruments to play round a campfire! (acceptable)

**3** Write sentences about the information in the table, using the words below to help you.

## A CLASS TRIP – WHERE WILL YOU GO?

|  | city | holiday resort | theme park |
|---|---|---|---|
| weather |  |  |  |
| price | €€€ | €€€€ | €€ |
| historic | ✔✔✔✔ | ✔ | ✔ |
| exciting | ✔ | ✔✔ | ✔✔✔✔ |

**0** weather / good / holiday resort / city

...The weather is better at the holiday resort than in the city..

**1** city / holiday resort / expensive

..................................................................................................

**2** theme park / expensive

..................................................................................................

**3** theme park / historic / holiday resort

..................................................................................................

**4** city / historic

..................................................................................................

**5** city / exciting

..................................................................................................

**6** theme park / exciting / holiday resort

..................................................................................................

**4** 👁 Correct the mistakes in these sentences or put a tick (✔) by any you think are correct.

**1** Smaller cities are more nicer than very big ones. ..........................

**2** She is one of the most important people in my life. ..........................

**3** Suddenly the man became more happy. ..........................

**4** Well, my bests friends are called Maria and Daniel. ..........................

**5** She is the most funny person I have ever known! ..........................

## VOCABULARY Prepositional phrases for location

**Look at this picture of an unusual house and write sentences about it. Use the phrases to help you.**

**0** on the tree

...There's a house on the tree....

**1** beside the house

..................................................

**2** above the house

..................................................

**3** behind the house

..................................................

**4** in the foreground

..................................................

**5** hanging from the tree house

..................................................

## LISTENING

**1** ▶5 **Listen to five conversations. What are they about? Choose the correct answer for each one.**

1 a description of the boy's house / how to get to the boy's house
2 a late dinner / arranging to collect someone
3 making an appointment / telling someone about different arrangements
4 where the family are going on holiday / plans for the weekend
5 a girl who doesn't understand her homework / a girl asking her mum some homework questions

### EXAM TIPS

**Listening Part 1**
- You have to choose the correct picture from a set of three. When you listen the first time, try to think about what the speaker or speakers are talking about.
- In the second listening, choose the picture that correctly answers the question.

**2** **Now read the questions and look at the pictures. Choose the correct picture, A, B or C.**

1 Where does the boy live now?

A  B  C

2 Where is the family going to buy dinner?

A  B  C

3 Why is the girl late for her dance class?

A  B  C

4 What does the boy have to take with him?

A  B  C

5 Which is Tessa's mum's favourite object?

A  B  C

**3** ▶5 ● **Listen again. For each question, choose the correct answer, A, B or C.**

## VOCABULARY Technology: nouns

**1** Write the letters in the correct order to make words. Complete the sentences.

1 TABTRYE

The ............................. on my phone has run out.

2 EETERPMINX

We're going to do an ............................. in chemistry tomorrow.

3 CIONCETONN

When there's a storm the ............................. is very poor.

4 ETVIONNIN

The best ............................. is the smartphone.

5 CHORT

You should take a ............................. with you if you go camping.

6 SLITTELEA

The information for the weather forecast comes from a ............................. in the sky.

7 LEFU

Mum is complaining about the price of ............................. .

8 ESCASC

You can ............................. the internet from the café: you just need the password.

9 MUPP

In some countries, there might be a village ............................. to get water from the ground.

10 EWORP

Turn off the ............................. at the main switch.

**2** Choose the correct answer.

1 It's a good idea to carry a *pump / satellite* on your bike at all times.

2 The *battery / fuel* that Dad puts in his car is good for the environment.

3 Sam hasn't got a very good internet *connection / access* at home.

4 There's no internet *access / power* where Jo lives – she has to do her homework in the library.

5 My *torch / battery* won't work. I think the switch has broken.

6 Uh oh! The lights have gone out again. It must be another problem with the *experiment / power*.

7 The first *satellite / experiment* went into space in 1957.

8 I've just read about an interesting *experiment / invention* involving an egg and two mobile phones.

9 The best *invention / connection* would be something that automatically does your homework for you!

10 There's something wrong with the remote control. I think the *power / battery* needs replacing.

**3** Read the short texts and write what these teens are talking about.

> I've had this since I was about 10 years old. It's red and my uncle gave it to me. I use it when there aren't any lights, or when I want to read at night and Mum has already told me to put my light out!

1 ........................................................................

> Everyone has at least one of these – they are in cameras, phones, clocks, computers, everything really. It's important that when they don't work any more that you recycle them. So don't just throw them out with the rest of your rubbish.

2 ........................................................................

> This is a piece of equipment that is sent into space around the Earth to collect information about the weather or used for communication.

3 ........................................................................

> Scientists and governments are always looking for new forms of this. This is because we are using too much of it, and we have to look for types that can be made again and again.

4 ........................................................................

> I've got one of these with my bike. When the tyres don't have much air in them, I use it. You definitely need one of these if you have a bike!

5 ........................................................................

## READING

**1** What is a *mobile device*? Choose the correct definition.

1 any piece of equipment

2 a piece of equipment that you can hold in your hand, usually electronic

3 a place where you can play computer games

**2** Look at these common devices. Tick (✔) the ones that are *mobile devices*. Why are the others different?

| | | | |
|---|---|---|---|
| mobile phone | ☐ | Wii U | ☐ |
| tablet computer | ☐ | Xbox | ☐ |
| laptop computer | ☐ | e-reader | ☐ |

**Reading Part 2**
- You are given descriptions of five people and each person is looking for three things.
- First, read the descriptions of the people and underline the things they want. Then read the longer texts and look for these things. They will be in different words and phrases.

**3** The teenagers below are all looking for a new computer game. Read and underline what they are looking for.

1 **Françoise** is looking for a game for her cousins to play online on their mobile phones and computers while they are all on a family holiday. Everyone wants to learn.

2 **Mark** is interested in a game with a good story. He wants to be able to play it on his own. He's keen on photography so good pictures are important.

3 **Esme** wants a game with animals involved for her five-year-old brother. He is skilled at using a mouse to control what he sees on screen and likes finding out about nature.

4 **Lily** is keen on changing what her characters wear. She would like a game where her actions decide what happens next as she loves being in control. She hasn't got a good internet connection.

5 **Frank** is interested in learning about other cultures. Being able to play with other people is important. He also loves discovering new music played on real instruments and knows a lot about that subject.

**EP Word profile** *actually*

**Match the sentences and the replies.**

1 Have you seen my sister? .......
2 Did you get the tickets? .......
3 Did I say we were going out on Monday? .......
4 You didn't tell me you needed to be at school early. .......
5 Do you like pizza? .......
6 Did Maria tell you? .......

a No, I couldn't believe it! They were actually all sold out.
b Well, I don't actually. I prefer pasta.
c No, she didn't actually say anything!
d No, actually, you said Friday.
e No, I haven't actually.
f Actually, I did.

**4**  Read the descriptions of the computer games and decide which one would be most suitable for each teenager.

 **A**

**Spellit!** A well-known word game that children and adults will love. You begin with a word and then build it up. Play it with friends – everyone has a phone! You must have a fast internet connection.

 **B**

**Tell Me Now!** This is no ordinary online quiz game. You'll learn so much that you didn't know. It's especially interesting if you like geography. You can play it together with your friends as long as you have an internet connection with you!

**C**

**Runway** is about a character that you create and adapt to many different situations. It's cleverly designed because you choose the result. It's all about the fashion style! It doesn't require the internet and you can play it alone.

**D**

Based on the children's story, **Fast Cars** is a great driving game. Play it with your best friend and sit comfortably as you drive around the city at night avoiding dangers. To really enjoy it, get some good headphones because the sounds are awesome!

 **E**

**Iron Iris** is the classic nightmare. Iris wakes up but she's not at home. You help her through a series of events and many dangers that she meets on her way home. It's an action game with levels for all ages, and the best thing is its amazing graphics. Play it by yourself anywhere.

 **F**

**Beach Fun** is all about the beach and includes several games. Younger children will enjoy helping to catch fish for the birds and playing ball with the dolphins. They will also learn a lot of interesting facts about the sea. No internet connection is necessary, but it's easier to play the games on a home computer.

**G**

**Grab the Treasure!** This is a basic mouse game. You can play it either online or offline. If you don't have an internet connection, though, you won't be able to share your results. You have to get your character around a garden. But be careful! Those cute-looking rabbits can actually lose you lives. It's a fun game and great for older children.

 **H**

**Round the World** is a family game for up to five players. You answer questions about typical songs, food and clothes from different parts of the world. There are other topics too. Also you create your character by choosing what it looks like. It's a fun game and has some great sound effects.

# GRAMMAR Future forms

**1 Choose the correct answers.**

1 Ask Jamie, *he'll / he's going to* help you with your project.
2 After school, *we're going to / we'll* hang out in the town centre. Come and join us.
3 Which of these devices *are replacing / will replace* phones by the year 2050?
4 I'm sorry but I'm not free on Monday as *I'm meeting / I'll meet* Sophia.
5 So, *I'm going to / I'll* tell you about the most amazing invention.
6 *We're uploading / we'll upload* all the new information to the website at midnight, as usual.

**2 Complete the conversations with the future continuous of the verbs in brackets.**

1 **A:** What will you be doing this time next year?
   **B:** ................................................. (study) even harder!
2 **A:** Do you think that Mr Jones has marked our work yet?
   **B:** Someone told me that ................................................. (do) it over the weekend.
3 **A:** Will you stay in touch while you're at your cousins' house?
   **B:** Yes, ................................................. (write) my blog every day.
4 **A:** I can't wait for the holidays to start!
   **B:** Same here! This time next week ................................................. (swim) in the sea!
5 **A:** Have you invited anyone to your party yet?
   **B:** ................................................. (send) a Facebook invite tonight!

**3 Read about Jyra and complete the text with the verbs in the correct future form.**

Tomorrow we ¹ ............................ (present) our ideas for technology in the future to the whole school. But first, some ideas! There are lots of exciting things that we think ² ............................ (happen) within the next five years. Over the next few years, scientists and inventors ³ ............................ (develop) new things for every aspect of our lives – the environment, communication, travel. It's likely that scientists ⁴ ............................ (find) fuels that are completely renewable. Also, it seems that they ⁵ ............................ (invent) cars that don't need any fuel at all!

As for communication, we all know about smartphones but did you know that next week Apple ⁶ ............................ (look at) 1,000 new apps. That's the number of apps that inventors send in every week! How ⁷ ............................ (our children/communicate) with each other? ⁸ ............................ (we/tell) them to stop looking at their phones? Who knows! It's the future and it's exciting!

**4 Complete the sentences about the future. Use a suitable future form and the words in brackets to help you.**

1 By 2050 we ...........................................................................
   ...........................................................................
   (drive / electric cars)
2 In the future people ...............................................
   ...........................................................................
   (wear / computers / arm)
3 We've already damaged the planet so we ................
   ...........................................................................
   (destroy / environment too)
4 Most people believe that we ...................................
   ...........................................................................
   (live / longer lives)

**5 👁 Correct the mistakes in these sentences or put a tick (✔) by any you think are correct.**

1 I bring the food and you bring something to drink.
   ...........................
2 I hope our relationship would last forever.
   ...........................
3 Give me a ring if you are coming. ...........................
4 Tomorrow we'll going to the pool and I know that will be a fantastic day. ...........................
5 At the weekend we go to a party. ...........................

# VOCABULARY enough, too, very

**1 Write the words in the correct order to make sentences.**

1 latest / isn't / The / very / phone / going to be / small
   ...........................................................................
2 expensive / apps / too / Some / just / are
   ...........................................................................
3 don't / in / mobile phones / long / last / Batteries / enough
   ...........................................................................
4 hasn't / got / Harry / to / go / money / enough / to the cinema
   ...........................................................................
5 was / first prize / win / to / slow / Svetlana / too
   ...........................................................................
6 tests / Next / are / important / term's / very
   ...........................................................................

**2 Complete the sentences with too, enough or very.**

1 Dylan is a ........................... good friend.
2 He's often ........................... busy to see me because he paints a lot.
3 His pictures are ........................... artistic.
4 His portraits aren't good ........................... for the competition.
5 They are ........................... strange for most people.

# WRITING   A short message

See Prepare to write box, Student's Book page 57.

**1** Look at the pictures. Do you own any headphones like these? Which type do you think are best?

**2** There is one mistake in each of these sentences. The mistake can be grammar, spelling, punctuation, word order or vocabulary. Correct the mistakes.

1  I'm go away for the weekend and
   I want to listen to my music.          ..........................

2  I think the green ones would be
   good – that's my favourite shape!     ..........................

3  Do you prefer the big headphones
   or the smaller ones.                   ..........................

4  I lost him at school last week.        ..........................

5  How long you have had your
   headphones?                            ..........................

6  I think that the sound is beter in
   the bigger headphones.                 ..........................

7  Most of my friends has the smaller
   ones but my headphones were too
   small and I lost them.                 ..........................

8  How do you chose your
   headphones?                            ..........................

**3** Read the task. Which three verbs tell you what you have to say in your reply?

.................. .................. ..................

> You want to buy some new headphones, but you need some advice. Write an email to your Australian friend, Lachlan. In your email, you should:
> **a** ask Lachlan for his advice on choosing headphones
> **b** tell him which ones you are thinking of buying
> **c** explain why you need them.
> Write 35–45 words.

**4** Look again at the sentences in exercise 2. Which ones match which part of the task? Write the numbers below.

a  ..........................
b  ..........................
c  ..........................

## EXAM TIPS

**Writing Part 2 (a short message)**
• There are three content points in Writing Part 2. You must cover all of these points.
• Make notes of one or two ways of answering each point before you write your final answer.
• Communicate your ideas clearly and keep to the word limit.

**5** Read this exam task. Write one or two sentences for each part.

> You are going to buy a new camera. Write an email to your English friend, Jim. In your email, you should:
> • tell Jim why you need a camera
> • give Jim some information about the model you are going to buy
> • ask Jim about the kinds of camera he and his friends have.

................................................
................................................
................................................
................................................
................................................
................................................

**6** 🔴 Now write your email.
• Remember to answer all the parts – use your ideas from exercise 5.
• Remember to check your spelling and grammar.
• Write about 35–45 words.

## VOCABULARY  Animals in danger

**1** Look at these photos. Choose a word from the box to label each one.

> creatures   crops   environment   humans
> jungle   landscape   population   rainforest

1 ...........................

2 ...........................

3 ...........................

4 ...........................

5 ...........................

6 ...........................

**2** Now match the words from exercise 1 to these meanings.

1 a tropical forest in which trees and plants grow very closely together ...........................

2 the number of people living in a particular area ...........................

3 anything that lives but is not a plant ...........................

4 a forest in a tropical area which receives a lot of rain ...........................

5 people ...........................

6 a plant e.g. grain, fruit or vegetable that is grown in large amounts ...........................

7 the appearance of an area of land, especially in the countryside ...........................

8 air, land and water where people, animals and plants live ...........................

**3** Complete the text with words from exercises 1 and 2.

When we think of Australia, we often think of beaches or the Sydney Harbour Bridge. But in the north of Queensland, there is a completely different ⁰ ...environment... that you can discover. This is the Daintree Forest. It is actually the largest area of tropical ¹ ........................... on the Australian continent and it is the oldest in the world. Very few ² ........................... live here; in fact the whole ³ ........................... of the area is only about 500 people. However, there are lots of other interesting ⁴ ........................... here, including the southern cassowary bird. The ⁵ ........................... includes mountains that go all the way down to the sea, where you can find some of the most beautiful beaches in the world. This area is really unusual in its plants and wildlife and now there are also large areas of ⁶ ........................... of cocoa, which is used to make chocolate. You'll taste the best chocolate here! So why not visit this amazing place which has something for everyone?

### EP Word profile *besides*

Write *besides* in the correct space.

1 My friend goes to bed early ........................... as she likes to read and ..........................., she's tired.

2 ........................... studying French and Spanish, ........................... Hans is studying Portuguese.

3 Mum and Dad lived in several places ........................... when they were young ........................... Paris.

4 There's Chinese food but ........................... the Chinese food ...........................there's also Italian food.

5 ........................... I don't want to go out tonight and ..........................., I have several pieces of homework to finish.

6 ........................... visiting our family, ........................... we usually visit friends over Thanksgiving.

# READING

**1** You are going to read about an event called *Clean Up Australia*. What do you think people do for this event? Tick (✔) one box.

| | |
|---|---|
| wear clean clothes | ☐ |
| wash other people's houses | ☐ |
| paint something in their house | ☐ |
| pick up rubbish | ☐ |

**2** Read the text quickly and check your answer to exercise 1.

## EXAM TIPS

**Reading Part 4**
- The questions in Part 4 have different purposes: the first and last questions are general – they test your understanding of the whole text.
- The other three questions test your understanding of detailed meaning in each paragraph of the text.
- Remember this when you are thinking about your answers.

**3** ● Read the text again and answer the questions below.

Grace Rees has recently taken part in *Clean Up Australia Day*. She spent the day picking up rubbish from a beach near her home. Grace has been involved in this event for about five years now. 'I've always done it with my school but this year my friends and I decided to register as our own group. We think it's good not only to pick up the rubbish but to bring to people's attention the fact that there is a lot of rubbish out there. If you do it with friends and family, then it means you can have fun and do something useful at the same time. It's an important thing to do. We have such a beautiful environment here and rubbish spoils it.'

The *Clean Up Day* event began in 1989. It was started by Australian Ian Kiernan, who had just sailed round the world and was shocked at the number of plastic bags and other forms of pollution in the world's oceans. So he decided to take action for something he felt strongly about.

The first *Clean Up Day* took place in Sydney and the following year it became *Clean Up Australia Day* with people all around the continent picking up rubbish. Every year more and more people take part. Today it is one of the most successful community events in Australia. In 2000 it became *Clean Up The World* and over 40 million volunteers from more than 120 countries took part. Every year a report of the day is produced containing a lot of figures, including the top ten rubbish items. Last year they included drink containers, sweet wrappers and small pieces of paper.

1 What is the writer doing in this text?
   A complaining about the lack of support for *Clean Up* days
   B giving information about an annual environmental activity
   C giving advice about keeping the countryside clean
   D reporting on the amount of rubbish in Sydney

2 What is Grace's attitude towards *Clean Up Australia Day*?
   A She thinks it's important to protect the natural world.
   B She sees it as an opportunity to take time off school.
   C She uses it as a way of spending time with her friends.
   D She doesn't like picking up rubbish.

3 Ian Kiernan began the event because
   A he had seen a lot of people with plastic bags.
   B he had just returned from an overseas trip.
   C he wanted to do something about rubbish.
   D he was worried about water quality.

4 The people who take part in this event
   A do it as their main job.
   B take time off work to do it.
   C give up their free time to do it.
   D love doing it.

5 Which comment about *Clean up Australia Day* best describes the event?

   A This is a great day for kids, especially if you like eating candy as there are all different types on sale.

   B It's a great day for the whole family to meet up and find out what's happened in the past year.

   C This is a day in Sydney when Australians think about the sailor Ian Kiernan and celebrate his ideas.

   D It's a day to think about the planet we share with others and to actually do something about it.

# GRAMMAR Conditionals: zero, first and second

**1** Write the words in the correct order to make sentences. Add a comma (,) in the correct place.

**0** won / If / the lottery / I / a boat / I / would / buy
*If I won the lottery, I would buy a boat.*

**1** I / If / a boat / another country / bought / would / I / sail / to

..............................................................................

..............................................................................

**2** I / sailed / visit / would / I / If / a lot of / places / different

..............................................................................

..............................................................................

**3** visited / I / If / a lot of / would / different places / I / photos / take

..............................................................................

..............................................................................

**4** I / If / took / put / photos / I / on my blog / would / them

..............................................................................

..............................................................................

**5** If / put / I / them / on my blog / my amazing trip / everyone / see / would

..............................................................................

..............................................................................

**6** win / if / very / But / the lottery / be / I / surprised / I'll

..............................................................................

..............................................................................

**2** Match the beginnings and endings of the sentences.

**1** If I go to Africa,
**2** If I won a million dollars,
**3** Unless you phone the bus company,
**4** If people recycle rubbish,
**5** If you threw the paper cups in the recycling,
**6** When Mark finds animals on the roads,
**7** If we had our own vegetable garden,
**8** If everyone turned off the lights,

**a** our electricity bill would be cheaper.
**b** he takes them to the vet.
**c** you won't get your umbrella back.
**d** we would save a lot of money at the supermarket.
**e** I'll go on a safari.
**f** there'll be less rubbish to bury.
**g** they'd become different paper products.
**h** I'd go round the world on a cruise.

**1** ....... **3** ....... **5** ....... **7** .......
**2** ....... **4** ....... **6** ....... **8** .......

**3** Complete the sentences with the correct form of the verbs in brackets.

**1** If you joined the basketball team, you .......................... (enjoy) it.
**2** If you ask Molly, she .......................... (help) you.
**3** If you don't do your homework regularly, you .......................... (fall) behind everyone else.
**4** When we go to the safari park, we .......................... (see) the big cats.
**5** If you heat water, it .......................... (boil) at 100°C.
**6** If I got the top mark in the class, I .......................... (be) very pleased with myself.
**7** If you wanted to help out, you .......................... (have) to sign up first.
**8** If you don't hurry, you .......................... (miss) the bus.
**9** .......................... you .......................... (mind) if I used your phone?
**10** When you press that button, the computer .......................... (turn) on.

**4** Complete the second sentence so that it means the same as the first.

**0** Unless we help animals in danger, they will disappear.
If ...*we don't help animals in danger*...............,
they will disappear.

**1** If he doesn't work hard, he won't pass the exam.
Unless ..............................................................,
he won't pass the exam.

**2** Unless it rains tomorrow, I'll play tennis.
If ..............................................................,
I'll play tennis.

**3** If you don't listen to the teacher, you won't know what to do.
Unless ..............................................................,
you won't know what to do.

**4** Unless we start growing our own food, we'll continue to spend a lot of money at supermarkets.
If ..............................................................,
we'll continue to spend a lot of money at supermarkets.

**5** If we don't do more to protect our environment, we won't be able to save more animals.
Unless ..............................................................,
we won't be able to save more animals.

**5** ⊙ Correct the mistakes in these sentences or put a tick (✔) by any you think are correct.

**1** I remembered if I don't find it they would not let me pass the class. ..........................
**2** Next weekend I have nothing to do so if you want, you can come to visit me. ..........................
**3** If you will go it will be better than it was.

..........................
**4** My parents would be very happy if you accept.

..........................
**5** I think if you met him you will like him. ..........................

## VOCABULARY   Phrases with *at*

**1** Match the phrases to their meanings.

1 at least ....... 5 at present .......
2 at first ....... 6 at once .......
3 at its best ....... 7 at long last .......
4 at all .......

**a** finally
**b** now
**c** immediately
**d** when you are telling someone about an advantage in a bad situation
**e** used for emphasis in questions or negative statements
**f** at the beginning of a situation or period
**g** at the highest level of achievement or quality

**2** Complete the email with phrases with *at*.

Hi Darcie!
The most amazing thing just happened.
I heard this loud bang and ¹ .............................
I didn't know what it was. I looked out of the window and I couldn't see anything unusual
² ............................ , so I carried on doing my homework. Then I heard the bang again and I ran downstairs ³ ............................ to get Dad. I wanted to know that he heard it too,
⁴ ............................ . He said, 'A bird has just flown into the window, twice! It's still a bit confused ⁵ ............................ but it's OK.'
We waited for about 20 minutes and then,
⁶ ............................ the bird flew off.
Write soon!
Sunny

## LISTENING

**1** Look at these photos. They were all in a competition called *The changing planet*. Which do you like best and why?

I like a / b / c best because ..........................................
.......................................................................... .

**2** You will hear a conversation between a boy and a girl who attended an exhibition showing the photos in the competition. What do you think they are going to talk about? Tick the topics.

the number of people there ☐
rainforests ☐
different types of camera ☐
people changing photos ☐
features of a good photograph ☐
how to take a good photograph ☐

**3** ▶6 Listen and check your answers.

### EXAM TIPS

**Listening Part 4**
• Read the six sentences before the recording starts – you have 20 seconds for this.
• Mark your answers in pencil at the first listening, choosing A for correct or B for incorrect.
• During the second listening, check you have the right answers.
• Remember that you will not hear the same words and phrases as in the questions – they will be said in a different way.

**4** Look at the first question and the part of the recording it asks about. Listen and <u>underline</u> the words that tell you the answer.

                                          YES   NO

1 Lindsay found the exhibition too
  crowded.                                 A     B

**Ben:**     What an exhibition, Lindsay!
**Lindsay:** I know, Ben! I loved it even if it was a bit busy – there was still enough space to look at the photographs. Weren't they awesome!

**5** ▶6 ● Listen to the rest of the conversation. Decide if each sentence is correct or incorrect. If it is correct, choose the letter A for YES. If it is not correct, choose the letter B for NO.

                                          YES   NO

2 Ben enjoyed the photos that
  were taken in a hot place.               A     B
3 Lindsay thought that the best
  picture was a water scene.               A     B
4 Ben suggested that Lindsay's
  favourite photo was changed
  in some way.                             A     B
5 Lindsay agreed that something
  was odd about her favourite
  photo.                                   A     B
6 Ben and Lindsay disagreed
  about how original the waterfall
  photo was.                               A     B

## VOCABULARY   School

**1** Write the letters in the correct order to make words.

1 DREGA .............................
2 RIPAMRY .............................
3 SCANDERYO .............................
4 QUONITACIFAIL .............................
5 GEDREE .............................
6 DEUNCATIO .............................
7 DETNAT .............................
8 REBKA   PU .............................
9 OD   LEWL .............................
10 OD   BLADY .............................

**2** Complete the sentences with the correct form of words from exercise 1.

1 Our teacher's name was Mrs Johnson and she taught us everything. I still remember story time at ............................. school.

2 I worked hard at university and I was really pleased with my result. I got a first class ............................. .

3 My birthday was never during school time. We always ............................. the week before.

4 The teachers always checked that everyone was in class. You have to ............................. school by law.

5 On the first day at ............................. school, we had about seven different teachers and classrooms.

6 We were in the seventh ............................. of school when we started learning biology.

**3** Complete the text with the correct form of words from exercise 1.

**Tell us how you feel about school**

When I was six, I went to [1] ............................. school. I enjoyed it because in first [2] ............................. , or year 1, everyone looked after us. We didn't have homework but we had to [3] ............................. in all our subjects, and the teachers helped us. At the age of 11, I changed schools and went to [4] ............................. school. That was hard because I didn't have any friends. I didn't like it and I [5] ............................. in the first tests. When we [6] ............................. for the holidays, I had to have extra lessons. I didn't want to go to school but I had to [7] ............................. . Fortunately, now I'm in Year 11 and things are different. These days I love school, have lots of friends, and I'm studying hard. I want to go on to university and get a first class [8] ............................. in design. It's really important to get a good [9] ............................. these days to find a good job. It just shows you how important [10] ............................. is!
*Jodie, aged 15*

## READING

**1** How many students are there in your school? Do you think it's a big school?

fewer than 500 ☐     500–1000 ☐
more than 1000 ☐

**2** Read the article quickly and complete the title.

### EXAM TIPS

**Reading Part 3**
- Be careful if you see the same words from the sentences in the text – you need to understand how they are used.
- Read the sentences again and underline the parts of the text where you find the answers.

**3** ⬤ Read the article again. Look at the sentences below and decide if each sentence is correct or incorrect. If it is correct, write A. If it is not correct, write B.

1 People usually call the City Montessori School by the initials of its name. .......

2 The first five students at the school were relatives of Dr Gandhi. .......

3 The school buildings are situated in several towns. .......

4 The head thinks it would be too difficult to organise a meeting of all the students. .......

5 The school has increased in size quite slowly. .......

6 Dr Gandhi recognises that many people have helped in the school's success. .......

7 The school fees are quite high and difficult to afford. .......

8 If a student is having difficulties at home, there is someone to talk to. .......

9 The school received a negative report from UNESCO. .......

10 The school sometimes has teachers and students from other countries. .......

# THE ............................ SCHOOL IN THE WORLD!

The first day at school can be quite scary for any pupil but imagine being one among 47,000! That is the total number of students at the City Montessori School in Lucknow, India. The school, better known as CMS, employs 3,800 staff including teachers, support staff, and others such as cleaners and gardeners.

The school was set up by husband and wife team Dr Jagdish Gandhi and Bharti Gandhi in 1959. The first pupils were the children of family members – and there were only five of them. As time went by, more people started to hear about the school and they wanted their children to attend. Slowly, the numbers rose. Today there are over 20 sites around Lucknow and the school's population is bigger than that of some towns. The school educates students between the ages of 3 and 17. They all wear a uniform and each class has about 45 pupils. But due to the size of the school, it is never possible for everyone to meet as there is no place that is big enough for everyone to fit in. The present head, Dr Gandhi's daughter Geeta Kingdon, said, 'The whole of Lucknow would be jammed if we tried because one bus holds 50 children, so we'd need 1,000 buses to bring everyone together.'

In 2013, the speed at which the school grew was recognised by the *Guinness Book of Records*. It was a proud moment for the school, and was because of the efforts of parents, pupils and teachers, said Dr Gandhi, who at the age of 75 is still involved in the school. The school doesn't receive any money from the government and the children's parents are only charged a small amount for their children to attend.

For each pupil there is also one teacher responsible for his or her health and life outside the classroom. In this way the staff believe that no one is forgotten. Besides the traditional subjects such as maths, English and geography, the students also learn about world peace. CMS is the only school in the world to be awarded a UNESCO Peace Prize for Education for its efforts in this field.

Today the school is famous for its exam results and its international exchange programmes. The school has some well-respected past students who have gone on to work in international organisations, but within the school, and especially with everyone wearing the same uniform, it can be difficult to get noticed so the students have to work especially hard. Dr Gandhi believes that the children receive not only an education but also a love of the world.

**4** Match the highlighted words in the text to the meanings.

1 the energy that you need to do something ...............................

2 have someone work or do a job for you and pay them for it ...............................

3 following the customs or ways of behaving that have continued in a group of people or society for a long time ...............................

4 happened or existed before now ...............................

5 feeling very pleased about something ...............................

EP **Word profile** *by*

**Complete the sentences with a phrase with *by*.**

1 I studied the poem last night. I know it really well. I know it ............................ .

2 The old ladies don't wash their clothes in a machine. They wash them ............................ .

3 I didn't mean to send you that text. I sent it ............................ .

4 The dog was on its own for about three hours. It was ............................ .

5 At home, I realised I had your book instead of mine. I picked up your book ............................ .

6 I've got your present! Wait for me outside school. Wait for me ............................ .

## GRAMMAR  Past perfect

**1** Complete the sentences. Use the words in brackets with the verb in the past perfect.

**0** When Max arrived home, his parents
...had taken his brother to the swimming pool...
(take / brother / to the swimming pool)

**1** Alice didn't want to go to the museum because she

.................................................................... .
(go there / on / school trip)

**2** Kelly wasn't allowed to do sports because she

.................................................................... .
(forget / trainers).

**3** Frank turned on his Xbox after he

.................................................................... .
(complete / all / homework)

**4** I gave Jenny a book for her birthday but she

.................................................................... .
(read / it)

**5** Kevin didn't have any homework because he

.................................................................... .
(finish / it / school)

**6** Luisa repeated the test because she

.................................................................... .
(not / do well / the first time)

**7** Mario was tired because he

.................................................................... .
(not / sleep / all night)

**8** When I got off the train at the station, my parents

.................................................................... .
(not / arrive / to meet me)

**2** Choose the correct answer.

Last week I ¹ *had / had had* a terrible day. First, I ² *woke / had woken* up late and so by the time I reached the bus stop to go to school, the bus ³ *already left / had already left*. Our neighbour was just leaving her house so she ⁴ *offered / had offered* to take me to school. Unfortunately, there was a lot of traffic and nothing ⁵ *moved / had moved* for about 30 minutes. I wanted to send my friend a text but then I ⁶ *realised / had realised* that I ⁷ *left / had left* my phone on the kitchen table. Finally, when I ⁸ *got / had got* to school, the bell ⁹ *didn't ring / hadn't rung* yet, which was strange. I went inside the school and looked at the clock in the school hall, and then I understood – the clocks ¹⁰ *went / had gone* back by an hour and so in fact I wasn't late at all!

**3** The short forms of *had* and of *would* are both: *'d.*
Does *'d* in these sentences mean *had* or *would*?

|  | had | would |
|---|---|---|
| **1** I'd like to go now. | ☐ | ☐ |
| **2** If I went there, I'd call you for sure! | ☐ | ☐ |
| **3** They'd just spoken to him. | ☐ | ☐ |
| **4** I'd just bought an umbrella. | ☐ | ☐ |
| **5** They'd met each other earlier. | ☐ | ☐ |
| **6** He'd do it if he had some money. | ☐ | ☐ |

**4** Complete the questions with the simple past or past perfect form of the verb.

**1 A:** Where ...........................................................
(you / meet) your new friend Jack for the first time?
**B:** On holiday in Spain.

**2 A:** What birthday present

...........................................................
(his parents / give) him a few weeks before?
**B:** A trip to Spain to visit his uncle.

**3 A:** ...........................................................
(he / ever be) abroad before?
**B:** Yes, once, to Florida.

**4 A:** ...........................................................
(his friends / not / organise) a party for his birthday?
**B:** Yes, a surprise party!

**5 A:** When ...........................................................
(they / tell) him that they had organised a party for him?
**B:** Two weeks before his birthday, when he told them about the trip to Spain.

**6 A:** How ...........................................................
(Jack / feel)?
**B:** Sad, because he wanted to do both things!

**7 A:** ...........................................................
(his parents / already / book) his flight?
**B:** Yes, and paid for it.

**8 A:** So what ...........................................................
(his friends / do) in the end?
**B:** They decided to have the party when Jack got back home, so he was very happy!

**5** ⊙ Choose the correct sentence in each pair.

**1 a** I went downstairs and found out my mum made roast beef.
**b** I went downstairs and found out my mum had made roast beef.

**2 a** After the match had ended, I had the opportunity to see the soccer players.
**b** After the match was ended, I had the opportunity to see the soccer players.

**3 a** That was my birthday present: my uncle had sent me a dog.
**b** That was my birthday present: my uncle send me a dog.

**4 a** When she got home, she happily found out that her parents bought her a puppy.
**b** When she got home, she happily found out that her parents had bought her a puppy.

**5 a** In the evening, she turned on the TV and realised that she had won the lottery.
**b** In the evening, she turned on the TV and realised that she won the lottery.

## VOCABULARY   Compound nouns

Complete the word puzzle, using the pictures.
What is the word reading down (↓) the grey boxes?

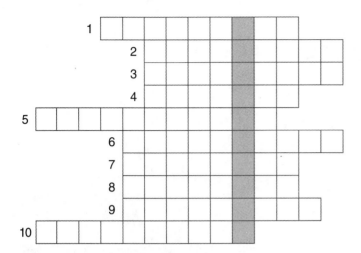

## WRITING   An email telling a story

See Prepare to write box, Student's Book page 67.

**1** How do you feel when you are going to take an exam or test?

> happy   sad   scared   frightened   nervous   excited

**2** Read Katie's letter and answer the questions.

1 What subject was the exam in?

...........................................................................

2 How had Katie prepared for the exam?

...........................................................................

3 What happened during the exam?

...........................................................................

4 Why did the teacher go red?

...........................................................................

Hi Jess,

I hope your exams are going well. I want to tell you about something that happened in an exam last week. It was so funny!

It was our end-of-year biology exam and we were all very nervous. I had studied really hard, but I really wasn't looking forward to it. The teacher read out the instructions carefully, but she didn't repeat what she had told us the day before: 'If your mobile phone rings, you will fail the exam.' Of course, we all looked at our phones and made sure we'd turned them off anyway!

We started the exam. Suddenly, a phone rang. Everyone looked around to see whose phone it was. Then we all noticed the teacher looking extremely red. We laughed so much! Even teachers forget things!

Love

Katie

**3** Read these sentences. Look at the adjectives or adverbs underneath them and choose the two that are possible in the space.

**0** The door started to open and everyone looked at it ..*excitedly / curiously*..

excitedly   curiously   differently

**1** She refused to put her bag on the

.............................................. floor.

delicious   dusty   dirty

**2** The people left the house

.............................................. .

secretly   quietly   completely

**3** My friend gave me a

.............................................. present.

painful   brand new   magnificent

**4** We walked into class

.............................................. .

nervously   extremely   quickly

**4** Your Canadian friend, Zac, is taking some important exams soon. He wants to know if you have any tips. Make notes.

Where do you study?

...........................................................................

How long do you study for?

...........................................................................

Do you do other things at the same time, e.g. listen to music?

...........................................................................

Do you have any other tips?

...........................................................................

**5** Write an email to Zac giving him your tips. Make it interesting with a short story if you can.

- Use adjectives and adverbs.
- Remember to check your spelling and grammar.
- Write about 100 words.

# 12 Getting around

## VOCABULARY Travel

**1** Label the picture with some of the words from the box.

| abroad | cruise ship | ferry | go away | harbour | land |
|---|---|---|---|---|---|
| on board | public transport | sail | set out | timetable | tourism |

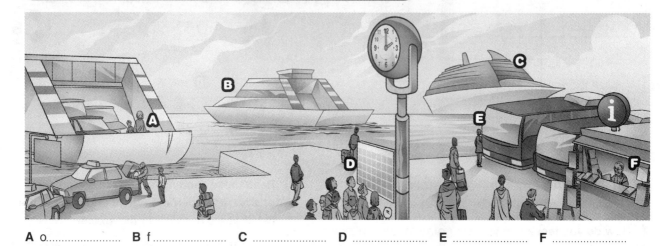

A o.....................    B f.....................    C .....................    D .....................    E .....................    F .....................

**2** Match the beginnings and endings of the sentences.

1 In the picture we can see one ferry leaving
2 A woman and a young boy are already
3 In the back of the picture there is a
4 In the front of the picture we can see
5 They are deciding which form
6 The old man gives people information

a on board the ferry.
b cruise ship arriving.
c of public transport to take.
d about tourism on the island.
e and another one arriving.
f some teens looking at a timetable.

1 ....... 2 ....... 3 ....... 4 ....... 5 ....... 6 .......

**3** Choose the correct answer.

1 When we had the World Cup in our country, ....... increased.
  **a** harbour  **b** timetable  **c** tourism

2 My friend Josh wants to study ....... next year and he's thinking about the USA.
  **a** on board  **b** abroad  **c** public transport

3 What time does your plane ....... ?
  **a** land  **b** check in  **c** sail

4 Many people get the ....... to work as it only takes ten minutes to cross the river.
  **a** cruise ship  **b** tram  **c** ferry

5 The girls ....... this morning at sunrise to catch the early ferry.
  **a** landed  **b** set out  **c** went away

6 Jane is ....... for a week and I'm looking after her cats.
  **a** going away  **b** setting out  **c** landing

7 Paul's grandparents live in a village with a lovely ....... , where all the fishing boats come in.
  **a** cruise ship  **b** harbour  **c** ferry

8 My parents want to ....... around the Greek islands on holiday this year.
  **a** set out  **b** land  **c** sail

## READING

**1** Which of these activities have you done on a beach holiday?

cookery classes ☐    water sports ☐
music classes ☐    learn a new language ☐
day trips ☐    shopping ☐

**2** ◐ The teenagers on page 49 are all looking for an activity to do on holiday. Read about the holiday resort and decide which activity would be the most suitable for each teenager.

## EXAM TIPS

**Reading Part 2**
- First, read about the teenagers and underline what they want. There are three things in each case.
- Then read the texts and underline activities that might be correct for each teenager.
- Finally, decide which activity would be the most suitable for each teen.

1 **Marta** only has a couple of hours to spare and wants to develop a skill involving live performances. She is also interested in how new technology is used in music.
2 **Josh** has to study every morning but wants to do something interesting in the countryside after lunch. He plans to surprise his parents by preparing a meal for them and needs advice.
3 **Zac** is keen to do something indoors involving computers with his two brothers. They enjoy anything that allows them to compete with each other and would also like to have a snack together.
4 **Judith** loves everything to do with water sports and is very good at diving. She'd like to do something active that lasts for half a day.
5 **Kacey** wants to see more of the area and learn about its wildlife. She's looking for a day trip that her sister and parents will also enjoy. They all love trying local food.

---

**A LANDSPORTS**

Whatever your game, we think we've got it. Beach volleyball lovers will enjoy playing on soft white sand or in the pool! We also have tennis that you can play on courts with spectacular views. And if it's your mind that needs to play, then we've got outdoor chess! Book in for two hours of fun.

**B TASTY**

Do you want to learn how to cook delicious dishes using local ingredients? We take you up to the mountains for a fun afternoon that will give you lots of new ideas and help with basic cooking skills. You're sure to please your family with the results!

**C ON THE SOFA**

Call in at our popular club and café near the harbour and enjoy free online access for as long as you want. We have a huge variety of games available that are suitable for all ages and skill levels. You can test your own ability or invite friends and family to play against you.

**D FLOCKO**

This is *the* place to hang out, for under 21s only. Watch the sunset with cool music playing as you enjoy some tasty pre-dinner snacks. Plan your next day's activities with your friends – new and old.

**E COOL OCEAN**

Home to some of the calmest, clearest blue seas in the area, we offer an incredible variety of activities, including windsurfing and sailing. Fly through the water powered by wind, an engine or your own power. Try something new or practise a sport that you love. Choose from morning or afternoon classes.

**F REMIX**

Train to be a DJ on the coast. Every day we run two-hour courses teaching you how to mix songs and become familiar with the latest computer programs for concerts and dance events. You will even be invited to make an appearance at our own club on Friday night!

**G DANCE**

Have you ever danced on a beach? Be more active! Come and learn new dance steps to great tunes every Wednesday. In the evening, we have dances where you can show everyone what you've learnt! A great experience for all!

**H OUT AND ABOUT**

Join us for an exciting adventure away from the resort, from 7.00 am until the evening. Experience deep-sea fishing, swimming with dolphins and an afternoon tour through the spectacular mountains, where you'll see lots of birds and butterflies. A tasty lunch on a farm is included in the price.

---

**3** Match the highlighted words in the text to the meanings.

1 something that happens to you that affects how you feel .............................
2 when the sun disappears in the evening and the sky becomes dark .............................
3 make someone feel happy .............................
4 extremely good, exciting or surprising .............................
5 very good, unbelievable, large .............................

**EP Word profile** *check*

**Complete the sentences with the correct form of *check* or a phrase with *check*.**

1 Jackie handed in her homework but she forgot to ............................. her spelling first.
2 I don't think that the ............................. desk is open yet.
3 We arrived at the airport too early and had to wait ages before we could ............................. .
4 There are so many security ............................. at airports these days.
5 We don't need to leave the hotel early so I'm going to see if we can ............................. this afternoon.

# GRAMMAR Modals (2): Obligation and advice

**1** Write full sentences using these words. Add any words you need.

**0** Janet / need / pay attention / more / class
....Janet needs to pay attention more in class.....

**1** If / you / go / France / should / buy / tourist guide
...........................................................................
...........................................................................

**2** Look / sign! / We / have / remove / shoes
...........................................................................
...........................................................................

**3** I / need / buy / more / paint / before / shop / closes
...........................................................................

**4** We / not / need / take / lunch tomorrow
...........................................................................

**5** You / shouldn't / take / photos / strangers
...........................................................................

**2** One answer is not correct in each sentence. Choose the two correct answers.

**0** If you have finished exercise 6 on page 7, you ....... do any homework.

  **(a)** don't have to   **b** shouldn't   **(c)** needn't

**1** You ....... buy your aunt a present; I've got something you can give her.

  **a** have to   **b** needn't   **c** don't have to

**2** I ....... finish this now – can we chat later?

  **a** need to   **b** have to   **c** shouldn't

**3** If you are feeling stressed, you ....... do some exercise. It really helps!

  **a** should   **b** needn't   **c** need to

**4** Mark ....... go to football practice at 7.00 pm – everyone is expecting him.

  **a** shouldn't   **b** has to   **c** needs to

**5** You ....... wait for me – I'd rather walk home.

  **a** have to   **b** don't need to   **c** don't have to

**3** Complete the email with modal verbs. Sometimes more than one answer is possible.

Hi Jessica,

I got your email last night about getting a visa to come and visit me in Australia. Firstly, you are right – you ¹ ........................... get a visa and you ² ........................... apply for that soon. You ³ ........................... leave it until a few days before you go! You ⁴ ........................... to worry about the cost because Mum is going to pay for you, but you ⁵ ........................... find out the address of your friends because that information goes on the form as well. You ⁶ ........................... show anything extra when you leave London – it's all done electronically.
See you very soon!
Sam

**4** Complete the caption under each sign with a suitable modal verb.

## HALF-PRICE FOR UNDER-15S

**1** If you're under 15, you ........................... pay the full price.

## STUDENTS' BICYCLES ONLY

**2** You ........................... leave your bicycle here if you aren't a student.

## GATE CLOSING IN 10 MINUTES

**3** You ........................... get to the gate within the next ten minutes.

**ALL LIBRARY BOOKS TO BE RETURNED BY END OF TERM**

**4** You ........................... give your books back to the library before the end of term.

**5** ⊙ Correct the mistakes in these sentences or put a tick (✔) by any you think are correct.

**1** You haven't to bring any food but you must bring a ball. ...........................

**2** You have to travel through the mountains on your bike. ...........................

**3** You will bring a coat because it's cold. ...........................

**4** It's going to be sunny so if you come, I think you should bring a hat. ...........................

# VOCABULARY Phrases with *on*

**1** Match the phrases with *on* to the meanings.

**1** on board   .......   **4** on purpose   .......
**2** on display   .......   **5** on sale   .......
**3** on foot   .......   **6** on time   .......

**a** not early or late
**b** on a boat, train or plane
**c** you can buy it
**d** walking somewhere
**e** arranged for people to look at
**f** intentionally

**2** Choose the correct answer.

**1** I used to go to school *on foot / on time*, but now I take the bus.

**2** The Year 12 art class have got their work *on purpose / on display* in the town library.

**3** As soon as we were all *on time / on board*, they closed the doors of the plane.

**4** This mobile phone is *on purpose / on sale* in most electronic stores.

**5** It was an accident – I didn't do it *on display / on purpose*.

**6** The class didn't start *on time / on board* because the teacher was late.

# LISTENING

**1** Read this advertisement and complete the notes below it.

## Do you know what to do if you lose your passport?

GenYTravel Tours is looking for young, experienced travellers to guide groups of young teens around the European cities. You should be a fun-loving, lively person with a university degree. You need to be responsible. We like our guides to speak at least one language as well as English. This would be a fantastic first job for someone who loves travelling.
Send your CV by 30 March. For more information click here.

Job: ..........................

Qualifications: ..........................

Languages: ..........................

Personal characteristics: ..........................

Apply by: ..........................

## EXAM TIPS

**Listening Part 2**
- Read the questions before you listen for the first time.
- As you listen the first time, try to get a general idea of the answer to each question and try to choose your answer.
- When you listen again, check your answers and also that the other options are wrong.

**2** ▶7 **You will hear an interview with Mike Finchley, who runs a travel company for young people. Listen to the interview and put the topics in order. Write 1–6.**

a looking after the teens ☐
b the best place to go ☐
c a surprising event ☐
d information on the website ☐
e education ☐
f a good suggestion ☐

**3** What is the connection between the advert in exercise 1 and the interview?

........................................................
........................................................
........................................................

**4** ▶7 ● **Listen to the interview with Mike Finchley again. Read the questions and choose the correct answer, A, B or C.**

1 How did Mike get the idea for his travel company?
 A from an enquiry he received
 B by taking different relatives on holiday
 C through readers of his travel blog
2 The first time people visit Mike's website,
 A they can select an experience that interests them.
 B they have to answer some personal questions.
 C they can see photographs of last year's holidays.
3 New Zealand is an example of a place that
 A can have two completely different programmes.
 B everyone wants to go to.
 C would be suitable for everyone.
4 The most important quality in the leaders is that they
 A know how to have fun.
 B have visited the places themselves.
 C understand teens.
5 The language tours include
 A traditional lessons in the classroom.
 B taking funny photographs.
 C real situations talking to real people.
6 The young photographer who won the competition
 A had taken many photography courses before.
 B got the photo that he really wanted.
 C waited a long time before taking the photo.

## VOCABULARY Photography and advertising

**1** Complete the word puzzle, using the clues on the right.

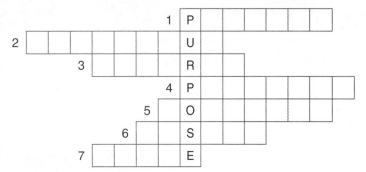

1 P _ _ _ _ _ _
2 _ _ _ _ _ _ _ U _
3 _ _ _ _ R _ _
4 P _ _ _ _ _ _ _
5 _ _ O _ _ _ _
6 _ _ S _ _ _
7 _ _ E _ _

1 something that is grown or made to be sold
2 a special way things are done
3 what companies put on TV between programs
4 place, where something is put
5 programs on a computer
6 when something happens because of something else
7 another word for picture

**2** Choose the correct answer.

1 Megan told me about an *advert* / *image* for a new clothes store with real people.
2 One form of advertising is to place a *product* / *software* on a TV show.
3 An *image* / *advert* is often stronger than words.
4 What was the *result* / *purpose* of that advert? It wasn't very clear.
5 Jon has developed his own *result* / *technique* for playing the game.
6 I bought a computer last week but I haven't installed any *software* / *results*.
7 The poster was the *result* / *position* of several hours' work.
8 Let's put the screen in that *product* / *position*, so we can all see it.

**3** Complete the information about a photo competition with the words in the box.

> advert    image    position    product
> purpose    results    software    technique

We are looking for the next generation of advertising photographers. You need to send us an ¹ ............................ of a piece of fruit or a vegetable, which will form part of an ² ............................ on healthy living. You can use any photo editing ³ ............................ program but we need to be able to view it on all mobile devices. The ⁴ ............................ of the piece of fruit or vegetable is very important – it should be clear and any leaves should be easily seen. The ⁵ ............................ of the photo is to sell a way of life, not a ⁶ ............................ . You can use a ⁷ ............................ that you are familiar with, or take the opportunity to try out a new one! The best ⁸ ............................ are often unexpected.

**4** Complete the speech bubbles in the cartoons.

Can you move the ........................ of your hand – place it behind your head!

I'm trying out a new ........................ today!

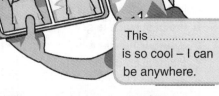

This ........................ is so cool – I can be anywhere.

I can't stand this ........................! I really don't know what it's selling.

# READING

**1** **Look at the photo of Jennifer Lawrence. Are these statements about her true (T) or false (F)?**

1 She is an Australian actor. ·······

2 She was the main actor in a successful film. ·······

3 She has a fit and healthy body shape. ·······

4 She is a fan of digital editing of body images. ·······

**2** **Read the text and check your answers to exercise 1. Ignore the spaces.**

### Improving images?

Everybody knows that digital software is **(0)** ....A..... to make images look different. People are **(1)** ........... to look taller and younger; legs become thinner and skin becomes clearer. **(2)** ........... there are sometimes extreme edits, **(3)** ........... celebrities actually admit this.

American actor Jennifer Lawrence has **(4)** ........... about this in public. She has talked about her body image and the demand to lose weight **(5)** ........... her lead role in the hit film *The Hunger Games*. Her character, Katniss, doesn't have enough to eat, so of course the film-makers wanted Lawrence to look **(6)** ........... . However, it seems that she **(7)** ........... to go on a diet. She also insisted that **(8)** ........... photography should not be used to achieve a similar effect.

Lawrence doesn't agree with photo **(9)** ........... that produce impossible images. Perhaps this is the beginning of a new **(10)** ........... of responsible celebrities.

**3** 🔵 **Read the text again and choose the correct word for each space.**

| | | | |
|---|---|---|---|
| **0 A** used | **B** worked | **C** done | **D** turned |
| **1 A** supposed | **B** changed | **C** moved | **D** known |
| **2 A** Because | **B** So | **C** Although | **D** Since |
| **3 A** some | **B** few | **C** little | **D** all |
| **4 A** spoken | **B** told | **C** said | **D** mentioned |
| **5 A** about | **B** of | **C** on | **D** for |
| **6 A** thin | **B** narrow | **C** small | **D** fine |
| **7 A** reserved | **B** disagreed | **C** refused | **D** warned |
| **8 A** clever | **B** comic | **C** qualified | **D** bright |
| **9 A** purposes | **B** results | **C** techniques | **D** skills |
| **10 A** family | **B** population | **C** team | **D** generation |

**4** **Choose the correct answer.**

1 Digital editing of images in films is usually used to *make actors look worse / improve actors' appearance*.

2 The film was *incredibly successful / not very successful*.

3 Jennifer Lawrence we*nt / didn't go* on a diet for her role in the film.

4 She believes that people *should see her as she really is / don't want to see her real image*.

5 Jennifer Lawrence is an unusual celebrity because she *complained about photo edits / wants to edit her own photos*.

🔵 **Word profile** *result*

**Complete these sentences using (a) result(s).**

1 We will know how our exam went on Friday.
We will know ...........................................
...........................................................

2 I was wearing winter clothes and I was too hot.
I was wearing winter clothes and as
...........................................................

3 We'll know the winner of the basketball competition later today.
We'll know ...........................................
...........................................................

4 The photographer used photo editing techniques and produced a better image.
The photographer used photo editing techniques and the
...........................................................
...........................................................

# GRAMMAR   The passive and modal passives

**1** Write the words in the correct order to make passive sentences.

1 computer / My / fixed / by / my / was / friend

....................................................................

2 films / A lot of / watched / laptops / on / are

....................................................................

3 an / prize / won / 11-year-old boy / The / was / by

....................................................................

4 stories / by / Most children / their / are / parents / told

....................................................................

5 computer / in the 1950s / first / invented / The / was / personal

....................................................................

6 injured / busy / Two / that / road / on / teens / were

....................................................................

**2** Choose the correct answer.

1 You shouldn't *take / be taken* photos of people with the sun behind them.
2 *You / The city* can be seen from here on a clear day.
3 *They must ride bicycles / Bicycles must be ridden* on the special path.
4 *Someone must warn people / People must be warned* that the beach isn't clean.
5 Under-18s *can use / can be used* this club.
6 Many apps *can download / can be downloaded* for free.

**3** Complete the modal passives with the verbs in the box.

> change   improve   make
> predict   upload   ~~use~~

Digital editing software can often ⁰ .....be used...... to change your appearance on screen. For example, your skin could easily ¹ ........................... to remove spots; the colour of your eyes could even ² ........................... from blue to brown. The final images can then ³ ........................... to a social networking site. So how can we ever be sure that something posted online is real? Does that matter? It is only natural for people to want to look good and every effort should ⁴ ........................... to achieve the perfect end result. Given the speed at which 3D technology is developing, future possibilities in this area can't ⁵ ........................... .

**4** Complete the text about the Kings Village Library. Use the words in brackets in the correct form of the passive.

The Kings Village Library is one of the oldest public libraries in the area. This library ¹ ........................... (build) in 1903. In 1987 it ² ........................... (move) down the street because it had gained so many books over the years. Today, children ³ ........................... (encourage) to join the library as soon as they can read. When anyone joins the library, a form ⁴ ........................... (must / complete). This form ⁵ ........................... (can / submit) online or in person. Competitions ⁶ ........................... (always / hold) on the last Monday of each month. For this month, teens ⁷ ........................... (invite) to be creative and share their work by entering the Fourth Annual Teen Poetry competition.

**5** ⊙ Correct the mistakes in these sentences or put a tick (✔) by any you think are correct.

1 We've been friends since he has born. ...........................
2 This game can be play online. ...........................
3 Well, my best friend called Julia. ...........................
4 The game can be played by two players.

...........................
5 I saw a school that make of wood. ...........................
6 I was given it for my birthday. ...........................

# VOCABULARY   Phrases with *in*

**1** Write the letters in the correct order to make phrases with *in*.

| | | |
|---|---|---|
| 1 VANCEDA | in | ........................... |
| 2 EFUTUR | in | ........................... |
| 3 LEGNEAR | in | ........................... |
| 4 RIARPUCALT | in | ........................... |
| 5 HET DEN | in | ........................... |
| 6 CFAT | in | ........................... |
| 7 LEADTI | in | ........................... |

**2** Complete the sentences with a phrase from exercise 1.

1 You should let the teacher know ........................... if you are unable to go on the school trip.
2 Read the application form ........................... – you don't want to miss anything.
3 All the dresses are lovely but I like the red dress ........................... .
4 ........................... everyone agreed on the party theme but it wasn't easy.
5 ........................... the weather in southern Europe is warmer all year than it is here.
6 Mercedes loved everything about the holiday: ........................... she said it was the best ever!
7 ........................... it would be better if you did your work on the computer. I can't read your writing.

## WRITING    A short message

See Prepare to write box, Student's Book page 57.

**1** Read these questions and choose the best answer for you.

1 Do you take lots of photographs?
 **a** yes, all the time
 **b** sometimes
 **c** hardly at all

2 How do you take photos?
 **a** with my phone
 **b** with a camera
 **c** with both

3 What do you mainly take photos of?
 **a** myself
 **b** my friends
 **c** other things

4 Do you share your photos?
 **a** yes – on social media all the time
 **b** from time to time – if there's a really good picture
 **c** not really – they're for me

**2** Read the task below. What should the writer explain to Chris?

.......................................................................

> You took some photos with a friend for a school project, but they aren't good enough to use.
> Write a note to your friend, Chris.
> In your note, you should
> • tell Chris about the photos
> • explain why they aren't good enough
> • suggest another time to take new photos.
> Write 35–45 words.

**3** The sentences are from the answer to the task in exercise 2. Number them 2–5 in the correct order.

**A** They're too dark and the colours aren't clear. ☐
**B** Hi Chris, ☐ 1
**C** Thanks, Burcu ☐
**D** I've looked at the photos and they aren't very good. ☐
**E** I think it's because the sun was in front of us. ☐

**4** Burcu didn't include one sentence. Which one is it? Choose the best sentence.

1 Can we meet tomorrow at 11am to try again? ☐
2 I am waiting for you tomorrow at 11am. ☐
3 Let's meet again! ☐

**5** Decide where the sentence should go and write out the note in the correct order. How many words is it?

.......................................................................
.......................................................................
.......................................................................
.......................................................................

**6** Now read Francesco's answer to the task. What is the main problem with it?

> Hi Chris,
> It was great to see you yesterday! We had a lot of fun taking photos!
> But the photos aren't very good. I looked at them this morning and they are really dark. I can't see you in some of them. I have no idea why that happened. Maybe you know? Maybe it was the sun. I don't think you should take photos when the sun is in front of you.
> Anyhow, I think we need to do them again. When can you meet? How about tomorrow after school?
> Your friend,
> Francesco

## EXAM TIPS

**Writing Part 2 (a short message)**
• Make notes of possible points for your answer and check the number of words in your notes. Make sure it is under the word limit.
• Write your answer to the question, using your notes.
• Count the words you use – make sure you keep to the word limit.
• Delete any details that aren't necessary if you have written too much.

**7** Read Francesco's answer again and delete any details which aren't necessary. Can you get the number of words down to 35–45?

**8** ◖◗ Now look at this task and write your answer.

> You took some photos when you were out for the day with your friend Sam, but you have lost all of them. Write an email to Sam.
> In your email, you should
> • apologise to Sam
> • explain how you lost the photos
> • ask whether Sam could send you some photos of the day.
> Write 35–45 words.

# 14 Ready to cook

## VOCABULARY  Verbs for cooking

**1** Look at the picture and complete the text with suitable verbs in the correct form.

In the picture we can see two teens getting ready for dinner. The boy is [1] ............................ some tomatoes in a pan on the cooker, and he's [2] ............................ them all the time. There's a kettle next to him, which is [3] ............................ . In the oven we can see a chicken, which is [4] ............................ . He's also preparing some toast, in the toaster, but it's [5] ............................! Outside, his sister is [6] ............................ some meat. Their friends are going to arrive very soon.

**2** Choose the two correct verbs in each list.

| | | | |
|---|---|---|---|
| 1 You do this with a spoon. | taste | stir | burn |
| 2 A way of cooking meat. | barbecue | bite | roast |
| 3 You do this with your mouth. | bite | fry | taste |
| 4 You do this over heat. | boil | roast | fry |
| 5 Something you can do to bread. | burn | fry | boil |
| 6 You can do this on a camp fire. | barbecue | roast | boil |
| 7 You can do this with garlic. | fry | roast | stir |
| 8 A way of cooking fish. | boil | taste | barbecue |

**3** Choose the correct answer.

1 Would you like to *bite* / *taste* this to see if there's enough salt?
2 Every Sunday we *roast* / *stir* a piece of meat for lunch.
3 I want you to *boil* / *stir* this sauce for me – don't stop!
4 Can you *boil* / *barbecue* some water for me, please?
5 Many people like the sound of *tasting* / *biting* into an apple.
6 Watch the pan and don't let the sauce *roast* / *burn*.
7 The first thing to do is to *fry* / *stir* some onions in a pan.
8 We should *stir* / *barbecue* these sausages now.

**4** Complete this recipe with the words in the box.

| boil | burn | fry | stir | taste |
|---|---|---|---|---|

1 ............................ the onion and garlic together and add some tomatoes.
2 Fill a saucepan with water, add some salt and ............................ .
3 Add some beef to the onion and tomato mixture and ............................ without stopping. Don't let it ............................!
4 Add the pasta to the water. When you think it is cooked, ............................ it to see if it is ready.

Enjoy your spaghetti bolognese!

## READING

**1** Read the website review quickly. What is the website about?

.................................................................................................

## EXAM TIPS

**Reading Part 3**
- As you decide on an answer, underline the part of the text that supports your choice – correct or incorrect.
- Do this for each question as you go along so that you don't get confused.
- Remember – the questions are in the same order as the information in the text.

**2** 🔵 Look at the sentences and read the review again to decide if each sentence is correct or incorrect. If it is correct, write A. If it is not correct, write B.

1 Claire Gourley's website is aimed at teens who already have some experience of cooking. .......
2 On Claire's website you can learn about health and safety in the kitchen. .......
3 Claire has invented all the recipes on the website herself. .......
4 Some of Claire's recipes are challenging to cook. .......
5 Claire's website offers some free training at a certain time of year. .......
6 If you do the course, you might learn how to save money in the kitchen. .......
7 Claire's videos contain some funny moments. .......
8 Claire's information about laying a dinner table is very basic. .......
9 Claire is only interested in getting photos of dishes that people have made. .......
10 Everyone who completes the course is sent a document showing their achievements. .......

### EP **Word profile** *keep*

Match the questions and sentences 1–5 to the replies a–e.

1 Why shouldn't I tell Rachel? .......
2 Why are you looking at your phone? .......
3 Did you get a birthday card from New Zealand? .......
4 This photo of your great-grandparents is about 100 years old. .......
5 Why did you start going to the gym? .......

a I want to keep fit.
b Wow! Can I keep it?
c She can't keep a secret!
d I keep hoping I'll get a text.
e I did! Kylie and I have kept in touch for ten years now!

## Review

Who does the cooking in your family? Do you know what makes a balanced meal? Nowadays, food programmes are in our homes almost every day – but what about helping teens to cook? We all know that this is an essential skill but how can teens get started? Eighteen-year-old Claire Gourley, from New Zealand, has developed a website that does just that.

Claire's website is called itsmyturntocooktonight.com and contains a range of useful information, like using a knife with care and checking that food is properly cooked to avoid making you sick! Claire says on her website, 'I'm here to share my food journey, to find out more about food, to discover cool kids' cooking ideas and kids' recipes, and of course to get some cooking skills so you can impress your friends and family!'

The website is divided into several parts and one of these is the recipe section. You'll find lots of suitable recipes which Claire has collected from different places, and which can be downloaded as an e-book. Claire says, 'I don't do complicated' and this is reflected in the recipes, which are always easy to make, taste great and are reliable. When she was putting her book together, she says that if the recipes didn't tick these boxes, she simply didn't include them!

Something that makes this website different from the many others available is its school holiday programme. For no charge, Claire has posted a set of online videos which teach you how to make delicious meals. And the course isn't just about recipes either. It includes information about making good food choices, explains how to read food labels and gives advice about spending less on ingredients.

The website feels fresh and teen-friendly, so it's no surprise that Claire loves to tell food jokes while displaying her cooking skills in the videos! The course also includes a few challenges for people, such as laying a table in the best way and working out what all the different-shaped knives and forks are for. Claire even suggests how to behave at the dinner table! All of these activities are designed to give teens practical skills and a deeper understanding of the food they eat.

At the end of the course, people are encouraged to upload photos of their own meals and favourite scenes from any dinner events they have organised. And they receive a certificate to prove they have taken part! All in all, a great website which is full of useful information and should be among the favourites of both parents and teens.

# GRAMMAR Non-defining relative clauses

**1** Complete the relative clauses with *who, which* or *whose*.

1 Food websites, ............................ often have easy recipes, are becoming very popular.

2 My best friend, ............................ love of food is well-known, always takes photos of her meals.

3 Martha Webster, ............................ is talking on TV at the moment, has her own website.

4 This cookbook, ............................ contains traditional recipes, was given to me by my grandmother.

5 Italy, ............................ food is just delicious, is where my parents are from.

6 Green smoothies, ............................ contain vegetables, are becoming popular.

**2** Complete the sentences with the correct phrases below. Use *which, who* or *whose* to make a single sentence.

> has just gone to university
> methods are actually quite hard
> my grandmother always made for me
> I had bought the day before
> husband makes wonderful meals
> is closed on Sundays
> ~~uses local produce~~

0 The restaurant near my house, ....*which uses*.... ....*local produce*................................... , makes excellent pasta dishes.

1 My mum's best friend, ................................. , ...................................................... has invited me to dinner.

2 This Australian Christmas cookbook, ..................... ...................................................... , is really a collection of summer recipes.

3 The shop near my house, ............................... ...................................................... , is running a special offer on sugar-free drinks.

4 My favourite dessert, ..................................... ...................................................... , has apples and cinnamon in it.

5 Jack chose a piece of fruit, ............................. ...................................................... , to put in his lunchbox.

6 Julia's older sister, ........................................ ...................................................... , has found a part-time job in an expensive restaurant.

**3** These sentences contain defining or non-defining relative clauses. Add commas where necessary to show the three non-defining relative clauses.

1 The book that I started reading at the weekend is really difficult.

2 My Auntie Netty who lives in Spain is a lawyer.

3 We're staying at the LaVida resort which Mum's friend recommended to us.

4 The man who lives across the street from my friend is a teacher.

5 The boy who is holding the ball is my cousin.

6 Darcie showed me a photo of her sister who is a ballet dancer.

**4** Complete the text about Jamie Oliver with *who, whose, that* or *which*.

Celebrity chefs [1] ........... are famous all around the world are not unusual these days. However, Jamie Oliver *is* different, and perhaps he is one of the most well-known celebrity chefs.

Jamie was working for a restaurant [2] ........... was famous in his home city of London when he was first noticed and invited to make a TV programme. His first TV programme, [3] ........... was shown in the UK in 1997, was called *The Naked Chef*. After the series, [4] ........... was a huge success, Jamie published a cookbook with the same name. It was bought by people [5] ........... came from all age groups and all kinds of backgrounds and became a number 1 bestseller.

Since then, Jamie, [6] ........... aim is to get people eating healthy food, has been involved in many other food projects, such as introducing healthy eating to people [7] ........... have very little money. He wants everyone to understand that eating healthily isn't expensive or complicated. But not everyone agrees and Oliver, [8] ........... is also now the owner of many restaurants and is very rich, has had to accept that not everybody thinks the same way as he does.

**5** ⊘ Correct the mistakes in these sentences or put a tick (✔) by any you think are correct.

1 There I met Jack, who is a very funny boy.

............................

2 We can visit São Paulo, that has a lot of great restaurants. ............................

3 It's about an astronaut whose spaceship gets attacked by aliens. ............................

4 Some new friends were sitting around the table were very friendly. ............................

5 Well, I have a friend that is called Manuel.

............................

## VOCABULARY Nouns often in the plural

**1** Add the missing vowels (A, E, I, O, U) to these words.

1 M ... M ... R ... ... S
2 ... N ... T ... ... L S
3 T ... ... R S
4 ... R R ... N G ... M ... N T S
5 ... N T ... R ... S T S
6 Q ... ... L ... F ... C ... T ... ... N S
7 ... N G R ... D ... ... N T S

**2** Match the words from exercise 1 to their meanings. Write the words.

1 the first letters of words/names ..............................
2 what you get when you are successful in an exam or course of study ..............................
3 things that you remember from the past ..............................
4 drops of water that come from your eyes when you cry ..............................
5 food used in the preparation of a particular dish ..............................
6 plans for how something will happen ..............................
7 things that you enjoy doing, studying or experiencing ..............................

## LISTENING

**1** Do you eat in restaurants? Do you cook? Complete the sentences so that they are true for you.

1 I usually eat at a restaurant
.................................................. .
(when? who with)
2 I make a meal at home for my family when
.................................................. .
3 My favourite meal is
.................................................. .

**2** ▶8 You will hear a conversation between a boy called Alex and a girl called Sian about planning a surprise meal for their parents. Which courses are mentioned? Do they agree?

starter ☐    main ☐    dessert ☐

**3** Look at the questions in exercise 4. What do they suggest you listen for? Match the questions to these functions.

1 agreement between the speakers ..............................
2 attitude (how a speaker feels) ..............................
3 opinion (what a speaker thinks) ..............................
4 suggestions ..............................

## EXAM TIPS

**Listening Part 4**
- Read the questions carefully and underline important words, such as verbs of attitude and opinion.
- Try to work out what each sentence is testing – an opinion, the agreement of both speakers, etc.
- Check all of your answers at the second listening, reading each sentence again.

**4** ▶8 ● Listen again and decide if each sentence is correct or incorrect. If it is correct, choose A. If it is not correct, choose B.

|  | YES | NO |
|---|---|---|
| 1 Alex accepts Sian's suggestion for a meal as a family. | A | B |
| 2 Sian suggests they look at recipe books for ideas. | A | B |
| 3 Alex and Sian agree that pasta is too plain. | A | B |
| 4 Sian thinks they should only use ingredients that they already have. | A | B |
| 5 Sian believes that the food's appearance is essential. | A | B |
| 6 Alex is confident that they can produce his choice of dessert successfully. | A | B |

**5** ▶8 Listen again and complete the sentences.

1 But ............................ ............................ a party, what do you think about a meal for just the four of us?
2 There, so let's choose the main first and ............................ ............................ that.
3 Simple is ............................ ............................ .
4 And this website says that the ............................ it looks is also really important!
5 How about some ............................ ............................ ice cream instead?

**6** Complete these sentences with the words you wrote in exercise 5.

1 Choosing a good main is ............................ ............................ at this restaurant.
2 ............................ ............................ jam is always better than shop-bought!
3 How about a starter to share ............................ ............................ one per person because they are quite big?
4 I hate it when the chef pays no attention to the ............................ the food looks.
5 Let's decide on our main course first and then we can ............................ ............................ desserts and starters.

# 15 City and countryside

## VOCABULARY   City and natural world

**1** Match the words to their meanings.

| | | | | |
|---|---|---|---|---|
| 1 | valley | ....... | 5 pollution | ....... |
| 2 | wildlife | ....... | 6 facilities | ....... |
| 3 | monument | ....... | 7 seasons | ....... |
| 4 | ruins | ....... | 8 clinic | ....... |

a the damaged parts of an old building

b an old building or place that is important in history

c the buildings, equipment and services provided for a particular purpose

d a place, often part of a hospital, to go for medical treatment or advice

e an area of low land between hills or mountains, often with a river

f the four periods of the year

g animals and plants growing independently of people in their natural environment

h damage caused to water, air, etc. by harmful substances or waste

**2** Complete 1–5 with the words in the box to make phrases.

> architecture   buildings   conditioning
> lights   spaces

1 historic   .............................

2 open   .............................

3 air   .............................

4 street   .............................

5 modern   .............................

**3** Complete the sentences with the phrases from exercise 2.

1 When it gets really hot, we turn on the
...................................................... .

2 I really like the way this town is set out because there are plenty of
...................................................... to walk in.

3 If you go to the countryside, you'll see lots of stars because there aren't any
...................................................... .

4 Some people really dislike
...................................................... because they say that it doesn't fit with older buildings.

5 If you want to see
...................................................... in Sydney, you should visit the Old Post Office and Central Railway Station.

**4** Choose the correct answers.

1

I really like spending holidays in Paris. I know that there's *pollution / seasons* because of the cars but I love visiting *ruins / monuments* like the Eiffel Tower. I love the mix of *modern architecture / facilities* and *historic buildings / street lights*.

2

I live in Switzerland and most people think of mountains but down in the *clinics / valleys* it is just as beautiful. You can see lots of *facilities / wildlife* like mountain rabbits, especially in the *open spaces / historic buildings*. At night we have a great view of the stars because there aren't any *street lights / facilities*.

3

Last year my family and I went to Egypt on holiday. We visited the pyramids and the ancient *ruins / clinics*. I loved Cairo because there are lots of *facilities / seasons* there for young people. It was summer though – the hottest *pollution / season*! I was glad our hotel had *air conditioning / facilities*.

## READING

**1** Read the text on page 61 quickly. Where does Phil live? Where did he visit?

......................................................................
......................................................................

### EXAM TIPS

**Reading Part 4**

• First, read the text quickly to get a general idea of its topic.

• Read the questions carefully and then read the text again, more slowly this time.

• Remember that words or ideas from the incorrect answers may also appear in the text.

**2** Look at question 2 and the second paragraph of the text. A student has underlined words connected to each answer to decide on the correct answer. What is the correct answer?

My son, Phil, has just returned from spending a week in the city with his cousin, Jed. We live in a small country town so it was interesting to hear what he thought about city life.

Firstly, Phil talked about the cost. He said <u>everything was too expensive, especially eating out in restaurants</u>. Every day the boys went into the centre but because Jed lives a 30-minute train ride out of town, <u>they didn't go home for lunch</u>. Fortunately, Jed knew some takeaway places that did <u>good food like salads and vegetable soups rather than burgers</u>. I don't think my son has ever tried so many different salads!

Phil missed the peace and quiet of the countryside a little, though the city traffic didn't bother him. He enjoyed being among all the people and saw that all Jed's friends were wearing expensive clothes with logos. At first he probably felt uncomfortable but then his cousin lent him some stylish trainers. I imagine that made him feel better. But he said that he had met teens his age who were dressed very differently. He liked the fact that in the city you could wear what you wanted.

As they began to run out of money, the boys had to find other things to do. Phil was amazed that there were so many free, or cheap, things available. For example, one lunchtime the boys walked into a museum where a band was playing modern music. They thought it was really good to hear a band inside a museum. What fun!

While I've always thought of my son as a country boy, he may want to spend some of his life in a big city after all!

**3** ⬤ **Read the text and the questions carefully. Choose the correct answer, A, B, C or D.**
Use the technique shown in exercise 2 to choose your answers for questions 3 and 4.

1 What is the writer doing in the text?
  A describing someone's opinions about a different experience
  B giving information about how to get around in the city
  C comparing living in the city and the countryside
  D warning teenagers against spending a lot of money in cities

2 What did Phil and Jed do for lunch?
  A They took the train back home.
  B They chose burgers and other fast food.
  C They ate in expensive restaurants.
  D They bought a range of healthy snacks.

3 During his time in the city, Phil felt
  A lonely without his family.
  B annoyed with the traffic noise.
  C embarrassed about his clothes.
  D frightened by the crowds.

4 What was so attractive about the music in the museum?
  A It was played by the museum staff.
  B It was beautiful old classical music.
  C It was one of many inexpensive activities in the city.
  D The museum's sound system was incredibly good.

5 What would Phil's father say about his son's recent experience?

  A Phil enjoyed staying with Jed and bought lots of new clothes in the city, but he prefers being in the countryside.

  B Phil was positive about his city break, and I wouldn't be surprised if he decided to move there for a while in the future.

  C Phil hasn't talked about his time in the city at all, so I'm not sure whether he liked it or not.

  D Phil was quite scared travelling around the city on his own, but his cousin recommended some interesting places he could visit.

**EP Word profile** *all*

Complete the sentences with the phrases in the box.

| above all   after all   all   all's well   and all that   at all |

1 I really like our new maths teacher and ............................ he's funny!
2 It was a beautiful day and there were no clouds ............................ .
3 The examiner asked us about our interests ............................ .
4 I didn't get a very good grade in my exam. ............................, I didn't have any time to study.
5 I hope ............................ when you get home.
6 I've got ............................ the shopping for the party.

# GRAMMAR Articles: *a/an, the* and zero article

**1** Complete the sentences with *a/an, the* or – (zero article).

1 Stuart is ........... car mechanic at ........... local garage.
2 ........... Statue of Liberty is in ........... New York.
3 ........... happiness doesn't come from ........... money.
4 Have you ever visited ........... capital of Sweden? It's beautiful.
5 Call ........... fire station! There's ........... fire!
6 I love these shoes. Are they made from ........... leather?
7 There's ........... mouse on ........... table in ........... kitchen.
8 Nobody saw ........... shark as it swam past ........... boat.

**2** Add articles to this text where necessary.

My mum is ²a̲ waitress in restaurant in city about 20 km from our home. She has worked at restaurant for 15 years but she wants to be teacher. At the moment she is studying in university in our town. She never complains about all homework. When she finishes university, we're going to visit USA. Then I think she'll decide on next course she wants to do!

**3** Read the text and decide which articles are correct. Correct the incorrect ones.

> ### Country Feature – New Zealand
> ᵀʰᵉ Country of New Zealand is in ᵗʰᵉ a̲ south-western Pacific Ocean. The country is made up of the islands, and it is called island country. It is situated about 1500 km east of Australia and about 1000 km south of the Pacific islands of New Caledonia, Fiji and Tonga. It is a long way from anywhere!
>
> People in New Zealand speak the English and Maori. A capital of New Zealand is the Wellington.
>
> New Zealand is famous for many things including its beautiful scenery which is made up of the mountains, the beaches and the volcanoes.
>
> There are many types of bird that can only be found in New Zealand including bird which cannot fly.
>
> Do you know anything else about this country which is so far from anywhere? Write to us at countrieswelove@ourspace.com.

**4** Complete the text with *a/an, the* or – (zero article).

## HOW MUCH TIME DO YOU SPEND OUTSIDE?

Do you live in [1] ........... city or [2] ........... countryside? With [3] ........... holidays coming up soon, two famous people are asking you to get outdoors. Adventurer Ben Fogle and top British cyclist Mark Cavendish have spoken about worries that [4] ........... today's kids spend too much time indoors in front of [5] ........... screen. [6] ........... online survey showed that only two in ten parents had taken their kids to look at [7] ........... stars, for example, or to go fishing. [8] ........... same survey also found that only a third of parents had gone for [9] ........... walk in [10] ........... hills with their children.

'From [11] ........... computer games to the lack of [12] ........... local green spaces, we have lost our sense of adventure a little as a nation,' said Fogle.

Meanwhile, Cavendish has asked [13] ........... kids to get on their bikes. 'Today's lifestyle … has made one of our most basic abilities – movement – [14] ........... option. I want to see more [15] ........... kids on their bikes.'

**5** ⊘ Choose the correct sentence in each pair.

1 a It was beautiful country.
　b It was a beautiful country.
2 a Do you have news?
　b Do you have a news?
3 a You have to survive in woods with nothing!
　b You have to survive in the woods with nothing!
4 a We can enjoy the nature and the fresh air.
　b We can enjoy nature and fresh air.

## VOCABULARY Phrasal verbs

**1** Write the letters in the correct order to make verbs.

1 OWHS .............................
2 AYTS .............................
3 CHACT .............................

4 DEN .............................
5 EMVO .............................
6 NOJI .............................

**2** Complete the sentences with a verb from exercise 1 and a preposition from the box below. You need to use one verb twice.

> around  in  in  in  out  up  up  with

1 I haven't seen Becky for a long time – I must ............................. her soon.
2 Tess had found an apartment and ............................. on Saturday.
3 I hate activities where you have to ............................. although you don't know how to play.
4 I think I'll ............................. this weekend and do all that biology homework.
5 After the movie, we went to Mickey's house and ............................. watching another movie!
6 It was my first visit to London and my cousin ............................. me ............................. .
7 My brother doesn't like his housemates and so he wants to ............................. .

## WRITING A blog post

See Prepare to write box, Student's Book page 89.

**1** Look at the heading of the *Answer a question* blog page and read today's question. Which do you prefer?

.............................................................................

> Answeraquestion@blogspot.com
>
> **Every day we ask you a different question: here is today's question! Tell us what you think!**
>
> ### Which do you prefer – the city or the countryside and why?
>
> [post #1 Sambeatboy]
>
> My cousin and I are really ¹ ............................. but we live in ² ............................. different places. He lives in the mountains and I live in the ³ ............................. city. We sometimes visit each other. When I was younger I liked playing in the ⁴ ............................. spaces and seeing all the ⁵ ............................. wildlife. ⁶ ............................. , nowadays, I find it ⁷ ............................. . ⁸ ............................. , I like it best when he comes to visit me in the city. We hang out in the city centre and he knows all my friends. ⁹ ............................. loving the countryside, he would like to study in the city when he is older. ¹⁰ ............................. , I think the best thing about the city is that you can find everything you want.

**2** Quickly read Sambeatboy's answer. Which does he prefer – the city or the countryside? Why? (Ignore the spaces.)

.............................................................................
.............................................................................

**3** Write the words from the box in the correct column in the table.

> actually  amazing
> boring  busy  close
> completely  despite
> finally  however  open

| Adjectives | |
|---|---|
| **Adverbs** | |
| **Linking words** | |

**4** Now complete Sambeatboy's post with the words from the table in exercise 3.

**5** You are going to write your own answer to the question in the blog. Write a few ideas for your answer.

**6** Now write down some more words you can use in the table in exercise 3.

**7** Write your blog post, using your ideas from exercises 5 and 6. Write about 100 words.

## VOCABULARY  Film

**1**  Complete the crossword, using the clues on the right.

**Across**

6  when you act, dance, sing or play music to entertain people
8  made with moving drawings, not real people
9  perform in a play, film
10  speech or music that is on a CD or sound file
11  seen or heard as it happens

**Down**

1  the person who tells the people in a film what to do
2  a person who makes films
3  become available (of a film) (4+3)
4  be in a play, film (6+2)
5  the process of making a film in which the models seem to move
7  tell the people in a film what to do
10  an actor's part in a film or play

**2**  Write the words in the correct column. Some may go into the table twice.

> act  animated  animation  appear in
> come out  direct  director  film-maker
> live  performance  recording  role

|  | Verb | Noun | Adjective |
|---|---|---|---|
| **Music/theatre** |  |  |  |
| **Film** |  |  |  |

**3**  Complete the text with words from exercise 2.

Last year the school drama group produced a play for all the parents. Mr Simms was the ¹ ............................ and he was great – he was very patient with the actors! I was one of the main actors, and my best friend Fiona ² ............................ the play as a cat in the first scene. There were songs too, and my little brother, Jonny, hadn't sung ³ ............................ before. He was really nervous! Mrs Fitzgerald made a ⁴ ............................ of the music about a week before – just in case! One of the scenes even included some ⁵ ............................ that the IT class had put together. We all had to learn to ⁶ ............................ and we had lunchtime classes with Ms Jones, the drama teacher. The last ⁷ ............................ of the play was a huge success and my parents really enjoyed seeing me in the lead ⁸ ............................ .

## READING

### EXAM TIPS

**Reading Part 2**

• Look for words or phrases in the text that mean the same thing as words and phrases in the questions.
• Some of the texts may have part of the information that you need. Only one text will have all the information – make sure it has the three things required.

**1**  ● The teenagers below all want to do a course. Read the descriptions of the eight courses at the community college on page 65. Decide which course would be the most suitable for the following teenagers.

1  **Alison** and her grandmother Nell both love working with cameras and computers, and want to do a course together every weekend. Nell can drive them to different locations.
2  **Jasmine** loves working on school plays and wants to learn more about technical things in the theatre. She needs a course at weekends where she can help on a local project.
3  **Artur** wants to improve the design of his blog and add some stylish effects. He'd like a course lasting a few hours, with extra work afterwards.
4  **Gabby** wants to invite her best friend on a full-day course as a present. They enjoy anything about clothes and personal appearance. Gabby wants to organise a birthday meal there.
5  **Nelson** wants to learn about developing online games on an evening course. He'd like to add music and animation to his own games site.

## CASTLE COMMUNITY COLLEGE – FOR PEOPLE YOUNG AND OLD!

### Courses at Castle Community College

### A LIGHT IT UP

Learn how to set up lights for a performance. We look at different positions for lights and their special effects, including the use of colour. During the course, you'll design and build the lighting for the town's Summer Show. There are ten weekly classes on Saturday mornings.

### B DIGITAL HELP

This course on Mondays (18.30–20.30) is for anyone who wants to explore their creative skills digitally, especially those who enjoy playing on the internet. We look at 3D technique, cartoon drawing, and how to make a model and bring it to life. There's also an opportunity to learn about music and video editing.

### C GET ACTING!

Do you enjoy being in school plays? This weekend course provides practical tips for future careers in the theatre or television, and helps you prepare for that important first role. This is a weekend course for anyone who wants to be a star! Meals and refreshments are included in the course fee.

### D BETTER IMAGES

Learn how to improve your photography or turn your old family albums into amazing digital books with easy-to-use software. The course includes some trips to beautiful places, where you'll get expert advice on taking better pictures. It is open to all ages and takes place on Saturdays over eight weeks.

### E ONLINE 2

This course continues from Online 1 (for beginners) and, like that one, offers excellent support material to work on following this half-day Saturday class. Building a website and communicating online isn't difficult these days – but we can suggest improvements to your website or online space, with help on technical things.

### F COMPUTER GAME DESIGN

Do you love playing computer games? Do you have ideas for your own games? If the answer to these questions is yes, then this course is for you. It is run in a nearby village two afternoons a week during the school holidays. You'll leave with a game designed by you!

### G PRODUCT PHOTOGRAPHY

You must have your own digital camera and be an experienced photographer to attend this practical evening course. Learn how to take high-quality photos of items such as clothes and make-up, for use online or in printed catalogues. Afterwards, you may be ready to earn some money!

### H FIND THE LOOK!

Do you know what looks good on you? Do you know how to choose the right make-up and hairstyle? On this fun Saturday, you'll get answers to all these questions, and more. We can arrange celebration lunches at the college too! There's a discount if two people come together.

---

**2** Look at the three things that Alison wants. Find all the words/phrases in the description of the courses that match them. Some of the courses don't have any information.

|   | working with cameras and computers | do a course together every weekend | can drive them to different locations |
|---|---|---|---|
| A |  |  |  |
| B |  |  |  |
| C |  | weekend course |  |
| D | photography, digital, software |  |  |
| E |  |  |  |
| F |  |  | nearby village |
| G |  |  |  |
| H |  |  |  |

**3** Why is course G *Product photography* not suitable for Alison?

.................................................................................

**EP** Word profile *direct*

**Match the questions and answers.**

1 Did you stop over in Singapore? .......
2 Can I help you? .......
3 What is Eliane doing now? .......
4 Is Jimmy still on the team? .......
5 Did Alison get good exam results? .......
6 Where are we going? .......

a No, he lost his place as a direct result of his poor performance last season.
b Yes, can you direct me to the post office, please?
c I think she's left acting and is directing at the local theatre.
d No, it was a direct flight.
e The old man directed us this way but I think we're lost again.
f She did and all as a direct result of her hard work.

## GRAMMAR   Reported speech

**1** **Write the words in the correct order to complete the sentences.**

1  Jack said … (was / directing / a / that / new film / he)
   Jack said ...............................................................
   ..................................................................... .

2  Amy said … (new film / just / out / her / had / come)
   Amy said ...............................................................
   ..................................................................... .

3  The newspapers said … (performance / the young actor / had / amazing / given / an)
   The newspapers said .............................................
   ..................................................................... .

4  He said … (each day / would / they / films / two / show)
   He said ..................................................................
   ..................................................................... .

5  The actor said … (more questions / could / that / he / answer / later)
   The actor said ........................................................
   ..................................................................... .

6  He said … (surprise / to hand out / gifts / had / some / also / he)
   He said ..................................................................
   ..................................................................... .

**2** **You have a new epal and you Skyped for the first time yesterday. Here are some things that Ana said to you. Now tell another friend what Ana said.**

0  I live in a small village with my parents.
   *...Ana said she lived in a small village*
   *...with her parents.*

1  In my free time I do aerial yoga.
   *...She said that*
   ................................................................

2  I'm learning two foreign languages at the moment, including Chinese.
   ................................................................
   ................................................................

3  I hope I can visit you next year.
   ................................................................
   ................................................................

4  I haven't visited an English-speaking country before.
   ................................................................
   ................................................................

5  I can play three musical instruments including the piano.
   ................................................................
   ................................................................

6  I'll send you a short video of my band soon.
   ................................................................
   ................................................................

**3** **Your friend says some things that are different from what she said before. Correct her, using the information in brackets.**

0  We're going to the cinema on Saturday evening. (afternoon)
   Really? You said ...*we were going on Saturday*
   *...afternoon.*

1  We're having pizza for dinner tonight. (sausages and potatoes)
   Are we? You said ..................................................
   ..................................................................... .

2  I borrowed a book from the library yesterday. (last week)
   Did you? You said ..................................................
   ..................................................................... .

3  My uncle doesn't like going to the cinema in the afternoon. (loved it)
   Really? You said ..................................................
   ..................................................................... .

4  My aunt will pick me up after football tomorrow. (dance class / Saturday )
   Really? You said ..................................................
   ..................................................................... .

5  Our friend Georgia has directed a short film. (acted in)
   Really? You said ..................................................
   ..................................................................... .

6  Jack has just uploaded his new film to YouTube. (uploaded / five weeks ago)
   Really? You said ..................................................
   ..................................................................... .

**4** ◉ **Correct the mistakes in these sentences or put a tick (✔) by any you think are correct.**

1  I answer that I like his idea. ...........................

2  She said that she love it very much.
   ...........................

3  The next month I received a call saying that I need to go and register. ...........................

4  She said that he dropped it on the bus early that morning so she gave it back. ...........................

5  He said that will help us expand our knowledge about things that are taking place around us.
   ...........................

## VOCABULARY   Reporting verbs

**1** **Match the reporting verbs to their meanings.**

1 insist    .......
2 announce    .......
3 demand    .......
4 explain    .......
5 suggest    .......

a make something clear to understand by giving details
b express a plan or idea for someone to consider
c tell people something officially
d say firmly that something must be done
e ask for something in a way that shows you do not expect to be refused

**2** **You heard this conversation in a gaming store. Complete the text below, reporting the conversation with the correct form of the verbs in the box.**

| | |
|---|---|
| **Marty:** | Hello, I bought this video game last week but I'd like to return it, please. |
| **Manager:** | Sure. What's the problem? |
| **Marty:** | It doesn't work properly. It keeps stopping. |
| **Manager:** | OK. Have you got the receipt? |
| **Marty:** | No, I haven't. |
| **Manager:** | You have to show me the receipt, I'm afraid. |
| **Marty:** | That's the problem – I've lost it. |
| **Manager:** | I'm sorry but I can't help you then. |
| **Marty:** | I'm not happy with that. I want to talk to someone else. |
| **Manager:** | Sorry, there isn't anyone else here. Why don't you write a letter to our head office? |

> demand    explain    insist    say    suggest    tell

Marty [1] ........................... that he had a game he
wanted to return. He [2] ........................... that it didn't
work properly. The manager [3] ...........................
that Marty should show him the receipt. Marty
[4] ........................... him that he couldn't show him
the receipt because he had lost it. The manager
apologised and said he couldn't help Marty, so Marty
[5] ........................... that he should talk to someone else.
The manager was on his own and [6] ...........................
that Marty could write a letter to head office.

## LISTENING

**1** ▶9 **You will hear an announcement about a competition. Listen to the first part of the announcement. What do you have to create?**

................................................................

**2** **In which order do you think these topics will be mentioned in the announcement? Write 1–5 – one topic is not mentioned.**

a entry date ☐
b what you have to do ☐
c who can enter ☐
d how long the clip has to be ☐
e why the competition is being held ☐
f prizes ☐

**3** ▶10 **Listen to the whole announcement and check your answers.**

## EXAM TIPS

**Listening Part 3**
- Some of the information you hear will be less important when completing the answers.
- Listen carefully for the answers and write the exact words you hear in the recording.
- Check your spelling at the end of the test.

**4** **Question 1 in the task below asks about the topic of the competition. Look at part of the announcement and find the answer. Delete any information about the topic that isn't necessary.**

Today, I'd like to tell you about this year's competition for the best video clip. We're taking part in a national project to use some of the 86,000 seconds or so that are in each day to help others.

Last year's topic was the environment and that was quite popular, though many of you said that it didn't give you much opportunity to show people in your video clips. So, this time we're putting them first and we'd like you to think about those who are disabled. Make an original and creative clip about this topic. For example, if every entrance to your school had wheelchair access, that would make a big difference, wouldn't it? So your video clip could look at an issue like that.

**5** ▶10 ● **Now complete the task. Listen again and fill in the missing information in the numbered space.**

> **SCHOOL COMPETITION**
>
> Topic for this year: *People who are*
> **(1)** ........................
> Closing date for entries: **(2)** ........................
> Entry conditions: *in* **(3)** ........................ *and under 18*
> Maximum length of video clip:
> **(4)** ........................
> First prize: **(5)** ........................
> Special winners' ceremony at
> **(6)** ........................

## VOCABULARY Verbs of communication

**1** Write the letters in the correct order to make words.

1 ESIGOLPOA ...........................
2 REMSIOP ...........................
3 RIMDEN ...........................
4 WRAN ...........................
5 KEJO ...........................
6 REWNOD ...........................
7 EEGIARDS ...........................
8 CAPLIMON ...........................

**2** Choose the correct answer.

1 Jake *apologised / promised* for calling at midnight.
2 Mum is always *complaining about / apologising for* the time I spend on social media.
3 Martine and I *wondered / joked* and laughed as we looked at photos of her as a baby.
4 Can you *disagree / remind* me to email you this photo of us when I get home?
5 Everyone in my class *joked / disagreed* with my opinion of the book.
6 I hate biology and I'm *wondering / warning* if I made the right subject choices last year.
7 Your sister *apologised / promised* to give me back the money I lent her last week.
8 The teachers *warned / complained to* us about the dangers of social media.

**3** Complete the text with the correct form of the verbs from exercise 1.

Yesterday I was studying when Mum ¹ ........................... me that our favourite TV programme was on. It's about teen–parent things and last night's was about social media. First, they showed a story of a lonely boy called Kyle who ² ........................... whether he would ever have any friends. Two boys in his class ³ ........................... about him online but it wasn't funny to him. In the end, one of the boys ⁴ ........................... but it was too late – Kyle had lost his self-confidence.
The programme also ⁵ ........................... us to be careful about the people you talk to on social media. Sometimes you don't know them and they might be dangerous. The next part was interesting. So many parents ⁶ ........................... about their kids using social media, telling them to turn the phone off at the table and so on. The film showed a mother who had no idea her daughter had friends all across the world! It's a great programme to watch with a parent because you will certainly ⁷ ........................... about some parts, and you can have a good discussion. But in the end, my Mum and I ⁸ ........................... to be more open with each other about online use.

**4** Look at the cartoons and complete the captions with the correct verbs from exercise 1.

I ........................... you! It's going to rain – take the umbrella.

I ........................... to love you forever.

I'm texting to ........................... because I can't come to your house later. We're shopping. ☹

I ........................... whether I'll have time to play football today.

# READING

**1** Quickly read the text about letter writing. Which of the following points are not made?

1 Writing letters is different from writing emails. ☐
2 Most people like reading emails again and again. ☐
3 You can keep letters. ☐
4 People are thinking about you when they write a letter to you. ☐
5 People who collect stamps write and receive a lot of letters. ☐

## EXAM TIPS

**Reading Part 5**
- Read the whole text first to get an idea of its meaning.
- Read the options and choose your answers.
- Read the text again with your answers in. Check that the whole text makes sense.

**2** ● Read the text below and choose the correct word for each space.

### Letter writing

It is unusual to get letters nowadays as **(0)** ....A.... of us prefer emails or texts. However, some people **(1)** ........... enjoy writing and receiving letters. Perhaps you would say that a letter is just **(2)** ........... an email? It is a kind of communication, but one important difference is that you can't **(3)** ........... an email in your hands immediately. In addition, you can put letters **(4)** ........... in a box to read again. When you do that, you will **(5)** ........... the writer, and maybe what you were doing when you got their letter.

This is **(6)** ........... different from emails, which we read quickly and then delete. There is something very **(7)** ........... in knowing that the person who wrote to you **(8)** ........... the time to stay in touch. Letters, **(9)** ........... updating you on exciting news, also send a clear message: the writer cares about you. In a fast and **(10)** ........... world, that is a wonderful feeling to share!

| | | | | | | | |
|---|---|---|---|---|---|---|---|
| **0** | **A** most | **B** few | **C** all | **D** lot |
| **1** | **A** already | **B** yet | **C** still | **D** even |
| **2** | **A** like | **B** as | **C** after | **D** with |
| **3** | **A** handle | **B** pick | **C** touch | **D** hold |
| **4** | **A** out | **B** through | **C** off | **D** away |
| **5** | **A** wonder | **B** remember | **C** think | **D** remind |
| **6** | **A** reasonably | **B** exactly | **C** completely | **D** directly |
| **7** | **A** special | **B** great | **C** certain | **D** excellent |
| **8** | **A** put | **B** left | **C** took | **D** kept |
| **9** | **A** towards | **B** besides | **C** along | **D** despite |
| **10** | **A** pulling | **B** turning | **C** breaking | **D** changing |

**3** Match the highlighted words and phrases in the text to the meanings.

1 certain or obvious ...........................
2 keep contact with someone by phoning or writing to them ...........................
3 the act of communicating with people ...........................
4 adding new information ...........................
5 remove something, especially from the computer's memory ...........................

## EP Word profile *know*

Choose the correct answer.

1 We've got a lot of studying to do, ........ .
  **a** I know    **b** you know    **c** as you know

2 Let's go to the same place as always – ........ it so well!
  **a** I know    **b** as you know    **c** I get to know

3 **A:** What are you going to wear to the party?
  **B:** ........ ! That new dress I got last week.
  **a** I know    **b** as you know    **c** you know

4 This is Fran – we ....... each other at summer school.
  **a** know    **b** as you know    **c** got to know

5 ......., my older brother has gone to study in the USA.
  **a** I know    **b** As you know    **c** You got to know

## GRAMMAR   Reported questions

**1** Write the words in the correct order to make reported questions.

**0** whether / wondered / a text message / received / she / had

Jessica

..wondered whether she had..

..received a text message.. .

**1** what time / to / his mum / wanted / know / collecting / was / him

Billy ..........................................................

.......................................................... .

**2** I / me / for breakfast / what / asked / wanted

Mum ..........................................................

.......................................................... .

**3** to / the phone / we / had / know / wanted / if / finished chatting / on

Dad ..........................................................

.......................................................... .

**4** cinema / the man / asked / which floor / the / on / was

The teens ..........................................................

.......................................................... .

**5** if / I / picked up / wondered / the post office / had / her parcel / from

Ms March ..........................................................

.......................................................... .

**2** Complete the reported questions. Make the necessary changes to pronouns, possessive adjectives and tenses.

**1** 'Are you ready to have dinner yet?'

Mum asked ..........................................................

ready to have dinner.

**2** 'Have you sent your aunt a text wishing her a happy birthday?'

Mum wanted to know

.......................................................... a text wishing

her a happy birthday.

**3** 'Have you listened to me at all today?'

Mum asked .......................................................... at

all that day.

**4** 'Do you think you'll hand in your biology project on Wednesday?'

Mum wondered ..........................................................

my biology project on Wednesday.

**5** 'Will you watch a film on your computer later?'

Mum wanted to know

.......................................................... computer later.

**6** 'Would you like to go to the cinema instead?'

Mum wondered ..........................................................

the cinema instead.

**7** 'Do you want to go for a pizza after the film?'

Mum asked .......................................................... for a

pizza after the film.

**3** Complete the conversation. Use the speech bubbles to help you.

> When did it happen?
>
> How did it happen?
>
> Is he badly hurt?
>
> Where is he now?

**A:** Mum, I told Michelle about Neil's accident. She asked [1] .......................................................... .

**B:** I think it was the day before yesterday.

**A:** Oh, and also, she wanted to know

[2] .......................................................... .

**B:** No, no one seems to know for sure.

**A:** She wondered [3] .......................................................... .

**B:** Well, he broke his arm, but it wasn't a bad break.

**A:** Ah, so is he at home now? Michelle asked

[4] .......................................................... .

**B:** He's still in hospital I think.

**4** 👁 Correct the mistakes in these sentences or put a tick (✔) by any you think are correct.

**1** They were new in our area and I want to know who they were. ..........................

**2** By chance he was in the park and I said him if he would like to play. ..........................

**3** I wonder what's inside the box so I open it.

..........................

**4** I saw him standing in the TV room, so I asked where does he come from. ..........................

## VOCABULARY   Adverbs of degree: *fairly, pretty, quite, reasonably*

**1** Choose the correct answer.

**1 A:** Did you see that programme about Facebook last night?

**B:** No, I was *very / quite* busy – I had homework for three subjects to do for today.

**2 A:** How was the English test?

**B:** It was *really / fairly* easy. I think I probably got about 60%.

**3 A:** What did you think of the restaurant?

**B:** The meals were *reasonably / very* cheap, but not as cheap as I'd expected.

**2** Put the adverb in brackets into the correct place in the sentence.

**1** It was noisy in the restaurant so I couldn't hear the musicians. (quite)

**2** I didn't have any lunch so I was feeling hungry by 3.00. (pretty)

**3** On the whole, Dad kept calm when I told him the news. (reasonably)

**4** Xanthe did well at school but not as well as her brother. (quite)

# WRITING    A story

See Prepare to write boxes, Student's Book pages 35 and 67.

**1** How can notes and messages affect us? Imagine that you receive the following messages. Write down an adjective to describe how you would feel about each one.

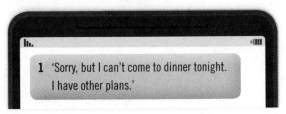

**1** 'Sorry, but I can't come to dinner tonight. I have other plans.'

From your best friend. You feel ............................. .

**2** 'Would you like to go to the cinema on Saturday afternoon?'

From a new friend. You feel ............................. .

**3** 'I've already asked you twice to clean up your room. Do it when you get home.'

From your mum. You feel ............................. .

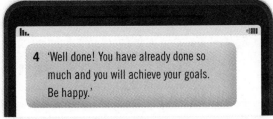

**4** 'Well done! You have already done so much and you will achieve your goals. Be happy.'

From *the Universe*. You feel ............................. .

**2** The last message is from a website called *Notes from the Universe*. If you join the website, it sends a message every day. Why do you think it does that?

1  to sell you something
2  to make your day a lovely day
3  to annoy you

**3** Read this story about a boy who received a message from the universe. Number the sentences in the correct order for the story.

The universe was right – something special happened! [8]

I wrote about losing her on a social media site. [ ]

It said something special would happen. [ ]

One day last week I received a message from the universe. [1]

A couple of days after I received the message, a girl contacted me to say she had found a cat like mine. [ ]

I said she was grey and white, and her name was Beauty. [ ]

I wondered what that would be because I had lost my pet cat the week before. [ ]

She emailed me a photo. It was my cat Beauty! [ ]

## EXAM TIPS

**Writing Part 3 (a story)**
*   Read the title or the first sentence of the story carefully.
*   If the pronoun is *I*, you need to write the whole story in the first person singular. If it is a name, or *he* or *she*, then you must write the whole story in the third person singular.

**4** Look at this exam task and make some notes to answer the questions below.

> Your English teacher has asked you to write a story. Your story must begin with this sentence:
> *Yesterday I received a message.*

What did the message say?
.........................................................................

Who was it from?
.........................................................................

Why had they sent it?
.........................................................................

How did you feel?
.........................................................................

What did you do?
.........................................................................

**5** 🔵 **Write your story.**

*   Use your notes from exercise 4.
*   Remember to check your spelling and grammar.
*   Write about 100 words.

## VOCABULARY   Feelings and qualities

**1 Match the adjectives to their meanings.**

| | | | |
|---|---|---|---|
| 1 annoyed | ....... | 7 nasty | ....... |
| 2 charming | ....... | 8 professional | ....... |
| 3 curious | ....... | 9 rude | ....... |
| 4 delighted | ....... | 10 shy | ....... |
| 5 lonely | ....... | 11 stressful | ....... |
| 6 mad (about) | ....... | 12 unexpected | ....... |

a  not expected

b  making you feel worried and not able to relax

c  quite angry

d  very pleased

e  wanting to know or learn about something

f  bad or unpleasant

g  unhappy because you aren't with other people

h  showing skill and careful attention

i  not confident, especially when meeting or talking to new people

j  loving someone or something

k  pleasant and attractive

l  not polite and upsetting other people

**2 Read the situation and choose the two correct adjectives.**

0  The woman got up, shouted at everyone and walked out.
(rude) / lonely / (unexpected)

1  That girl is always on her own. She doesn't talk to anyone.
lonely / charming / shy

2  The woman I work for is so nice. She is helpful and I'm learning a lot.
professional / annoyed / charming

3  I was the only person in our group who did the work. It was hard.
annoyed / nasty / stressful

4  I just love scarves! Thank you so much for the present!
delighted / mad about / rude

5  I wanted to know what would happen next so I looked and spoilt the story!
annoyed / curious / shy

6  I can't believe the way he spoke to you. That's awful.
nasty / rude / charming

**3 Choose the correct answer.**

1  Last week I had an *unexpected / annoyed* visit from my best friend, Billy. It was so nice.

2  The girls' mother was *charming / shy*. She listened to what we said and made nice comments.

3  Martha is *nasty / mad* about the latest fashion for plastic bracelets.

4  The boy was *delighted / shy* with the present his parents gave him – a new phone!

5  I was *rude / curious* to know what would happen next in the book.

6  The way that woman spoke to my dad was just *stressful / rude*.

**4 Choose the correct adjectives from exercise 1 to complete these news items.**

Prince Albert of Monaco is said to be
[1] ............................. about a film that has just been made about his mother, Princess Grace. It seems that some of the Grimaldis are [2] ............................. and would like to keep their lives private.

Australians have recently been [3] ............................. by another royal, Prince George of the United Kingdom, and by his [4] ............................. smile. Yesterday he had fun at Taranga Zoo in Sydney.

Emma Watson is [5] ............................. in many aspects of her life – a good role model for young people. In 2014 she graduated from university, and two of her films came out – almost certainly a [6] ............................. year with all that work, but what an achievement! Go Emma!

## READING

**1 Read the text on page 73 quickly. What is the TV programme about?**

1  a famous person

2  people with famous brothers and sisters

3  unhappy children

### EXAM TIPS

**Reading Part 4**

• Read the text quickly to get a general idea of what it is about.

• Remember that the three middle questions are in the same order as the information in the text.

• The final question asks about the general meaning of the text – about the text as a whole.

# FAMOUS BROTHERS AND SISTERS

Dr Todd Payne has recently made a documentary about people with famous brothers and sisters. He has studied these relationships for many years and was invited to make a documentary about them. 'It's such an interesting area,' he said, 'because, surprisingly, what these people feel may be no different from the rest of us.'
The documentary begins with a general look at brothers and sisters, and he makes the point that everyone argues, everyone occasionally feels that they want what their brother or sister has, for example, the present which we think is not as 'good' or as 'big' as our brother's or sister's present. This is all part of our need for attention – our parents' attention. But with a famous brother or sister in the house, things can become more complicated.
In one part we see two young children, Peter and Alex, walking to school. An adult is behind them but it's not clear who this person is. Then, suddenly, more security men appear as photographers jump out to get a picture of Alex, who is a child actor. How would Peter feel? asks Dr Payne. No one wants *your* picture. And if you're in the picture, you'll be edited out.
This, however, is not Jacki Pelangi's opinion. Because of her famous sister, a singer, she has seen amazing shows, eaten in great restaurants and had a lot of designer clothes! She doesn't mind her sister's celebrity because she has had experiences that most people only dream of.
At the end, we are left with the idea that people are people. Some people hate having a famous member of the family, others love it, and some even become famous themselves!

**2** ● Read the text again and the questions below. For each question, choose the correct letter, A, B, C or D.

**1** What is the writer doing in this text?
  **A** complaining about rich and famous people
  **B** advising how to become a singer
  **C** reporting on a TV programme
  **D** describing the lives of one family
**2** What point does the writer make about brother–sister relationships?
  **A** Arguments within a family are usually helpful.
  **B** Everyone wants to be brought up in the same way.
  **C** Younger children aren't satisfied with their presents.
  **D** People with a famous brother or sister might disagree with them more.
**3** What does Dr Payne suggest about Peter's feelings?
  **A** Peter would probably prefer to walk to school alone.
  **B** Alex's behaviour makes him unhappy.
  **C** Peter is likely to be upset by the photographers' actions.
  **D** The security men make Peter feel scared when they appear.
**4** What is Jacki Pelangi's opinion of having a celebrity sister?
  **A** She wishes that the two of them got on better.
  **B** She complains that she can't go anywhere on her own.
  **C** She is jealous of her sister's experiences.
  **D** She feels that it has given her great opportunities.

**5** Which comment best describes the documentary?
  **A** Having a famous brother or sister is horrible – Dr Payne will tell you why and how you can deal with this situation.
  **B** The programme shows that people with famous brothers and sisters rarely ask them for help.
  **C** Dr Payne explains how relationships between famous brothers and sisters are usually very similar to those between ordinary brothers and sisters.
  **D** Children with famous parents can't go anywhere without people wanting to take their photo and they are unhappy about this.

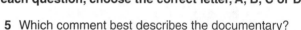

**EP** **Word profile** *quality*

**Match the sentences to the replies.**

**1** Did you enjoy the food at the new café?  .......
**2** Do you think I should be a teacher?  .......
**3** Can you come over on Sunday for a chat?  .......
**4** This has broken already!  .......
**5** Have you marked my work yet?  .......
**6** What's the best thing about me?  .......
**7** I'm going to visit Auntie Louisa.  .......
**8** Why did you pay so much for that?  .......

**a** Yes, you have the right qualities!
**b** Saturday would be better for some quality time.
**c** I'm not surprised. It was such bad quality.
**d** Yes, they only use quality ingredients.
**e** You have so many good qualities!
**f** Yes, and it's very good quality. Well done!
**g** It wasn't a lot really and it is high quality.
**h** That's a good idea. It's good to spend quality time with family.

**3** **Who are the following people?**

**1** Todd Payne  .............................................................
**2** Alex  .............................................................
**3** Peter  .............................................................
**4** Jacki Pelangi  .............................................................

## GRAMMAR *have something done*

**1** Complete the sentences, using the correct form of the words in brackets.

**0** Maureen ............................................. by her friend. (hair / cut)
Maureen ........... has her hair cut ........... by her friend.

**1** Mark ............................................. by the local bike shop. (bike / repair)

**2** My mum ............................................. by the village baker last year. (my birthday cake / bake)

**3** Jeff ............................................. by a pavement artist every year. (picture / paint)

**4** We ............................................. last year. (our house / paint)

**5** Mum ............................................. by professional people. (her bedroom / decorate)

**6** I ............................................. by the dentist. (a tooth / fill)

**2** Rewrite the second sentence, using *have something done*.

**0** This morning they parked my car outside the garage.
........ This morning I had my car parked ........
........ outside the garage. ........

**1** They took my picture yesterday.
.............................................

**2** They have cut and washed my hair.
.............................................

**3** They prepared the food for me.
.............................................

**4** They are going to make my new jacket.
.............................................

**5** They have cleaned my shoes.
.............................................

**6** They are going to update our website.
.............................................

**3** Look at the pictures. What have the people had done? Use verbs from the box to write sentences.

cut   deliver   fix   repair   take

**0** ...... He's had his hair cut very short. ......

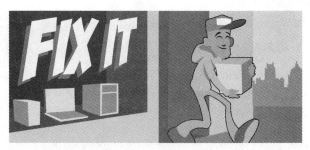

**1** .............................................

**2** .............................................

**3** .............................................

**4** .............................................

**4** ⊙ Choose the correct sentence in each pair.

**1 a** I was happy to see him there and I asked him to take a photo with me.
**b** I was happy to see him there and I asked him to have his photo taken with me.

**2 a** I'm going to the dentist's to have my teeth checked.
**b** I'm going to the dentist's to checking my teeth.

**3 a** In Madame Tussauds I had pictures with Arnold Schwarzenegger and James Bond!
**b** In Madame Tussauds I had pictures taken with Arnold Schwarzenegger and James Bond!

**4 a** I have to see the doctor and have my body checked.
**b** I have to see the doctor and have to check my body.

## VOCABULARY Prepositions

**1 Complete the sentences with *to* or *of* if necessary.**

1 According ........... Janet, it's going to rain tomorrow.

2 What do we need to take on the school trip besides ........... our lunch?

3 Despite ........... having two projects to do, I'm still going to watch the football!

4 My favourite singer is doing two concerts because ........... his huge number of fans.

5 Regarding ........... the test next week, remember to arrive at school half an hour early.

6 Let's study at your house tomorrow instead ........... mine.

**2 Complete the dialogue with the prepositions from exercise 1.**

**Mum:** When are you going on your Year 10 geography trip, Julie? [1] ........................... the information here, we need to pay for it now. Is that right?

**Julie:** I think so. But did I tell you that [2] ........................... staying at the Rose Hotel, we're now staying at the Holiday Place?

**Mum:** Oh, why's that?

**Julie:** I think that [3] ........................... the time it would take to get to the area that we have to study, the teacher thought it was better to stay closer. And [4] ........................... the location, it's cheaper.

**Mum:** OK, that's good. Is there anything else [5] ........................... the trip I need to know?

**Julie:** No, I think that's it! I'm really looking forward to it [6] ........................... the weather forecast – rain! Ugh!

## LISTENING

**1 Look at the six sets of pictures. What do you think each conversation is going to be about? Write a few words under each one.**

**2 ▶11 Listen and check your answers.**

### EXAM TIPS

**Listening Part 1**
- You will hear each recording twice.
- The first time you should listen to get a general idea of the topic and choose your answer if you can.
- The second time you listen, you should listen carefully to check your choice.

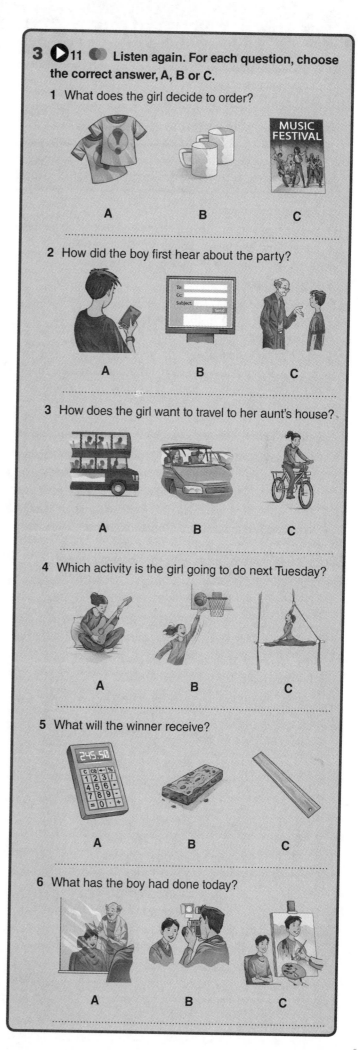

**3 ▶11 Listen again. For each question, choose the correct answer, A, B or C.**

1 What does the girl decide to order?

A        B        C

2 How did the boy first hear about the party?

A        B        C

3 How does the girl want to travel to her aunt's house?

A        B        C

4 Which activity is the girl going to do next Tuesday?

A        B        C

5 What will the winner receive?

A        B        C

6 What has the boy had done today?

A        B        C

## VOCABULARY   Work tasks

**1** Match the words in the box to their meanings.

> arrange   calculate   deal with   deliver   develop   handle
> install   manage   organise   produce   run   update

1 add new information .....................................
2 take things such as goods, letters and parcels to people's homes or places of work .....................................
3 understand and take action in a difficult situation .....................................
4 discover an amount or number using maths .....................................
5 plan or prepare for something .....................................
6 make the necessary plans for something to happen .....................................
7 be in control of an office, shop, team .....................................
8 make something new over time .....................................
9 make or grow something .....................................
10 put a piece of equipment somewhere and make it ready for use .....................................
11 take action in order to achieve something or in order to solve a problem .....................................
12 control something, e.g. an event .....................................

**2** Read the sentences and choose the two correct answers.

1 Jason's dad *runs / manages / produces* a small Thai restaurant in our town.
2 Mr McKenzie had to *calculate / deal with / manage* a large number of complaints about the new school café.
3 I thought Mr McKenzie *handled / dealt with / organised* the complaints about homework really well.
4 The IT people are coming next week to *update / install / arrange* the school computer system.
5 Who is going to *calculate / produce / update* our class blog this week?

**3** Complete the blog post with the correct form of verbs from exercise 1.

> http://www.itsallaboutme.myblog.com
>
> Guys, guess what!! I got the holiday job.
> I'm so excited! The woman who runs
> the shop – Mrs Ford – asked me when I
> could start work! It's going to be great – I
> have to ¹ ........................... with people,
> ² ........................... newspapers to a few
> homes and ³ ........................... some orders –
> you know, work out how many things we need
> and how much they cost. She asked me if I
> could ⁴ ........................... some upgrades to
> her computer (easy!) and then she wants to
> me to ⁵ ........................... a local newsletter
> online. I have some time to do it – it's not
> immediate but it'll be mine! I'll be the person
> who ⁶ ........................... it. Also, we're going
> to ⁷ ........................... a healthy milkshake
> afternoon (so no sugar!) for the primary school
> kids when they get off the school bus. I'm
> excited! I'll have to ⁸ ........................... my time
> really well.
>
> *Posted by Marina on Monday at 2.02pm*

## READING

**1** Read Marina's blog post quickly. Which jobs did she do on her first day?

.............................................................................................
.............................................................................................

**2** Read the blog post again and answer the questions.

1 What are the dress rules for the shop/café?
.............................................................................................
2 What job did Marina like best on her first day?
.............................................................................................
3 What will the café give her?
.............................................................................................
4 What does she want to learn?
.............................................................................................

Just completed my first Saturday at work and it was so cool! There's a uniform, which everyone has to wear, which is a black T-shirt with the shop logo on and black trousers or a skirt. There are also rules for hair and I was reminded that I have to wear mine tied back at all times.

There were four of us working in the shop today and everyone was so pleasant and helpful to me, especially when I had to ask questions about where things are. The manager asked me to produce a list of all the items on the food shelves, which was a bit boring, although at least I know where things are now!

After our lunch break, I saw that the noticeboard was looking very messy so I removed the notices that were out of date, and moved the others to make them look more attractive. It took quite a bit of time but I enjoyed it and in the end I was pleased with the result. (I've put a photo up.) Finally, I was allowed to work at the counter, taking money from customers, which was a bit stressful.

The manager, who is also a friend of my mum's, said that I had worked hard all day. In fact she's so pleased that next week I've been asked to work in the café. I'm delighted because I'll gain some really useful experience and I'm hoping that someone will teach me how to make those pretty patterns on cappuccinos!

*Posted by Marina on Saturday at 8.24pm*

## NOTICEBOARD

1 Ballet classes cancelled today due to illness. Tomorrow as normal unless we contact you.

2 Hi, I'm a 14-year-old girl available for babysitting weekends and early evenings.
I've completed my school first-aid certificate and have experience of babysitting under-5s.
Phone Joanne on 7493845.

**3 BASKETBALL CLUB**
Monday's competition starts at 6.30 pm.
Be here one hour before for practice.

**4 CHANGE TO FREE SCHOOL BUS**
Now collects from station rather than library.
Still 7.30 am.

**5 SNACK MACHINE OUT OF ORDER**
Sandwiches and crisps can be bought in café.

**3** ⬤ **Look at the text in each notice. What does it say? Choose A, B or C.**

1 A If you can't come today, contact the office to book another class.
  B If you don't hear from us, your class will take place tomorrow.
  C If you cannot attend your class due to illness, please let us know.

2 A Joanne is able to look after young children at the weekends.
  B Joanne is willing to babysit late at night if necessary.
  C Joanne is free to teach first aid in the evenings.

3 Players in the basketball competition should
  A practise before they come to the club.
  B be ready to do some practice at 6.30 pm.
  C arrive at the club in advance for practice.

4 Which arrangement has changed?
  A the time when the bus leaves
  B the place where students can board the bus
  C the charge to students for using the bus

5 A The café is only selling hot meals today.
  B A new snack machine has been ordered.
  C You cannot use the snack machine today.

## EXAM TIPS

**Reading Part 1**
- Read the texts carefully and think about where you might see them, and why they are there.
- Read the questions; there are three options for each one.
- Look for words and phrases in the questions that mean the same as words and phrases in the notices.

## EP Word profile *order*

**Match the sentences to the replies.**

1 Has the waiter taken our order yet?   .......
2 I didn't order a pizza and salad!   .......
3 Why are you working every weekend?   .......
4 I can't find that book I was telling you about.   .......
5 Is this machine out of order?   .......

a In order to earn some money for my holiday.
b Why don't you keep your books in alphabetical order?
c Yes, sorry. The repair man is coming now.
d No, it's a bit slow here.
e Sorry, that was for another table!

## GRAMMAR Different types of clause

**1 Choose the two correct linking words.**

1 I have to go to bed earlier *as / because / while* I have to catch an early bus tomorrow.

2 Matthew never took notes in class, *although / in order to / whereas* his brother took lots.

3 Can you pass me my glasses *so that I can / because / in order to* read this form?

4 She seems really easygoing, *while / whereas / because* she's actually pretty difficult.

5 I can pick up some milk *although / as / because* I'm going past the shops on my way home.

6 Last year I went to the USA *in order to / so that I could / because* go to my cousin's wedding.

**2 Complete the sentences with the beginnings or endings below. Use *although*, *as* or *so that* to join the two parts.**

> your work will be mainly in the shop
> I enjoyed the party
> I'm not going to have a starter
> the teacher can explain the rules to you
> I have football practice
> ~~she can improve her grades~~

0 She's going to study harder ...so that she can.......... improve her grades............................. .

1 ................................................................................
   I didn't know anyone.

2 You should arrive earlier on the first day .....................
   ............................................................................... .

3 ................................................................................
   ................................................................................
   we might need you in the café too.

4 ................................................................................
   ................................................................................
   I want to have a dessert!

5 I'll be home late tonight ........................................
   ............................................................................... .

**3 Complete the text with the correct linking word from the box. More than one may be possible.**

> although    because    in order to    so that    whereas

I have the best job in the world! But I'm not going to say what it is [1] ............................. this is a game and you have to guess. I'll give you a few clues [2] .............................
you can work it out. It wouldn't be a fun job for someone who didn't like dealing with customers, especially little kids. I usually work at the beach and [3] .............................
get something to eat, you'll probably come and visit me. Some people know what they want; they choose from 100 flavours quickly [4] ............................. others can take forever!
You're on holiday and have all the time in the world, [5] ............................. I'm working and time is money!
**What's my job? I'm a(n)** ............................. .

## EXAM TIPS

**Writing Part 1**

- Read the task instructions and the five first sentences quickly to get a general idea of the topic.
- Read each second sentence with your answer in place, to make sure that it means the same as the first sentence.
- Never write more than three words.
- Remember that there can be more than one way of completing the answer.
- Check you have spelt your answers correctly.

**4 ⬤ Here are some sentences about a boy's Saturday job at a sports centre. For each question, complete the second sentence so that it means the same as the first. Use no more than three words.**

0 Pierre was given a Saturday job at the sports centre recently.
   The sports centre .......gave Pierre....... a Saturday job recently.

1 Pierre's a very good swimmer so he was given the job.
   Pierre got ................................. he's a very good swimmer.

2 They needed people so that they could look after the young swimmers.
   They needed people in ................................. look after the young swimmers.

3 Pierre says that he loves swimming but he hates working out in the gym.
   Pierre says that ................................. hates working out in the gym, he loves swimming.

4 Pierre's reason for wanting a Saturday job was to save money for a diving course.
   Pierre wanted a Saturday job ................................. he was saving money for a diving course.

5 Pierre's a strong swimmer but he can't dive well, which is strange.
   It is strange that ................................. Pierre's a very strong swimmer, he can't dive well.

**5 ⊙ Correct the mistakes in these sentences or put a tick (✔) by any you think are correct.**

1 I like her because she's very friendly although she is too strict with me. .............................

2 Now I have to go my mother is calling me to eat.
   .............................

3 I'm writing to tell you about last weekend as you asked. .............................

4 She looked down for not get distracted and said, 'I know, I know.' .............................

5 I like Stefanie while she is a very kind, friendly and confident person. .............................

## VOCABULARY   *as* and *like*

**Read about these jobs and complete the text with *as* or *like*.**

1   There are lots of young people who are working
............ bloggers. They write about things that interest
them ............ fashion or food. This experience of
writing online, and having followers and reading other
people's posts, can in fact be excellent experience for
many jobs ............ writing for a newspaper.

2   I work in a high street shop on Saturday mornings. It's
OK but I'd like to do something more interesting ............
my friend Luis, who works at the library. He says it's
boring but I think it would be wonderful to work ............
a junior librarian because I love books! I'm known in
my school ............ *Bookie* because I read so many
books! But I don't care – I love reading!

## WRITING   An informal letter

See Prepare to write box, Student's Book page 111.

**1   Below is a list of tasks that you might have to do
in a part-time job. Write a job from the box or add
your own idea next to each task.**

> shop assistant     hairdresser's assistant
> working in a café/restaurant     newspaper boy/girl

1   organising the shelves                    ...........................
2   making an appointment                  ...........................
3   calculating the change to give
     a customer                                    ...........................
4   dealing with enquiries                    ...........................
5   delivering goods                             ...........................
6   making a reservation                      ...........................
7   developing the social media            ...........................
8   handling difficult customers            ...........................
9   cleaning the floor                           ...........................
10   serving customers                         ...........................
11   organising an event                       ...........................
12   updating an advertisement            ...........................

**2   This is part of a letter you receive from your
Australian friend, Elise. Make a list of part-time/
holiday jobs people your age might do in your
country.**

.......................................................................................
.......................................................................................

> For my homework project, I have to write about
> different jobs that young people do in different
> countries. What jobs do young people do in your
> country? What skills and experience do these
> jobs give them?

**3   Read this reply and tick the points in Connor's
plan below that he included.**

> Hi Elise,
> In my country there are lots of opportunities for
> young people to work although they are mainly at
> the weekends. We have a lot of school work to
> do during the week!
> Many of us work in shops on Saturdays. You
> can get a job in a clothing store or sports shop
> in a shopping mall. In the summer, there are
> jobs on the beach. If you're a good swimmer,
> you can help if people get into trouble. Working
> develops important skills like talking to people
> and handling difficult situations.
> I think having a part-time job is great because
> you learn skills and make new friends.
> Best wishes,
> Connor

> * list of jobs e.g. waiter, working in
>    a fruit shop                                                     ☐
> * how much we earn                                           ☐
> * where we work                                                 ☐
> * what we get from the work                              ☐
> * why we work                                                     ☐
> * how many hours per week we work              ☐
> * when we work                                                   ☐
> * jobs we want to do in the future                     ☐

## EXAM TIPS

**Writing Part 3 (an informal letter)**
* Make sure you develop the ideas in your letter.
* Use informal language throughout.
* Check your answer for correct spelling and grammar.

**4   This is part of a letter you receive from your friend,
Kyle. Make some notes to answer the questions.**

* If you have a part-time job, write to Kyle and tell
  him all about your job.
* If you don't have a job, think of a job you would like
  to have and then write your letter to Kyle.

> We're doing a project on different ways of
> spending Saturdays around the world. I know you
> have a part-time job. What would be your perfect
> part-time job?

**5   ⬤   Write your letter.**
* Write in an informal style.
* Write about 100 words.
* Remember to check your spelling and grammar.

# 20 Making plans

## VOCABULARY Hopes and dreams

**1** Find the words in the word square (→ ↓ ↗ ↘) to match the meanings.

1 succeed in something good, usually by working hard .......................

2 find someone or something attractive, or respect them .......................

3 intend to do something .......................

4 decide to do something .......................

5 think of something that you would like to happen .......................

6 make someone more likely to do something, make them more confident .......................

7 try to get or do something .......................

8 have an idea of something in your mind .......................

9 continue to do something, or do it again and again .......................

10 make the greatest effort possible .......................

| D | H | Y | R | L | P | Q | F | E | B | S | Z |
|---|---|---|---|---|---|---|---|---|---|---|---|
| O | Y | H | K | M | F | A | V | G | D | W | T |
| I | M | A | G | I | N | E | J | X | R | S | C |
| K | P | H | O | Y | I | L | W | R | E | N | B |
| K | E | T | S | H | C | V | Y | B | A | S | G |
| E | D | B | C | G | H | W | R | A | M | M | I |
| E | Z | A | I | M | O | U | U | L | P | H | F |
| P | M | D | J | L | O | F | A | B | T | R | D |
| O | O | M | I | Y | S | S | O | X | P | H | F |
| N | L | I | Y | E | E | N | L | R | K | S | G |
| Z | C | R | B | O | K | L | T | E | V | M | Q |
| F | T | E | N | C | O | U | R | A | G | E | I |

**2** Choose the correct answer.

1 My grandfather *dreamt* / *chose* of being an airline pilot.

2 I *encourage* / *aim* to go on to university and study history.

3 Who do you think has *achieved* / *admired* more – the inventors of Google or Facebook?

4 Michelle *kept on* / *went for* practising the same tune but she still couldn't play it properly.

5 This boy at school has *achieved* / *encouraged* me to join the basketball team practice on Fridays.

6 We told our teacher that we had *kept on* / *tried our best* at the athletics competition.

7 Next year we have to *choose* / *aim* which subjects to do for the exams.

8 Older people can't *aim* / *imagine* how hard we have to study these days.

**3** Read this talk that a teacher is giving his class just before the end-of-year exams. Complete it with the correct form of the verbs in exercise 1.

'OK, class. Listen, everybody! Before the exams start on Monday I just want to say a few things. I guess that you are all ¹ ....................... of getting good marks? Well, you may be, but it's just as important to ² ....................... in everything you do. Here are some ideas to help you revise. First, I would ³ ....................... you to write out a plan for the subject you're studying and then find a quiet place to work. If I were you, I'd ⁴ ....................... to study for about three hours at a time but have a break every 20 minutes or so. Not many of us can ⁵ ....................... studying for longer. Personally, I ⁶ ....................... people who can concentrate for long periods, but most of us need a rest from time to time. If you find that you are unable to ⁷ ....................... much, then try not to worry. Have a break and come back to it feeling fresh. Then you'll be able to ⁸ ....................... it! Try to ⁹ ....................... yourself holding that piece of paper with your exam result on – it reads 'excellent', right? It's up to you – you just have to ¹⁰ ....................... to succeed!'

## READING

**1** Look at the animals in the article on page 81. Write their names below.

.......................  .......................

**2** Read the article quickly. How did the girls become successful with their animal businesses?

......................................................................
......................................................................
......................................................................
......................................................................

## EXAM TIPS

**Reading Part 3**

- Read the questions carefully so that you know what you are looking for in the text.
- Remember, the ideas from the sentences will be in different words in the text.
- Underline the words that you think give you the answer and check them carefully when you have answered all the questions.

## 3 Look at the sentences below. Read the text and decide if each sentence is correct or incorrect. If it is correct, write A. If it is not correct, write B.

1 Naomi started working with animals from a young age. .......

2 The woman who sold her the first guinea pig was important in starting Naomi's business. .......

3 Naomi's brother refused to help her in the beginning. .......

4 Naomi concentrates on her guinea pig business full-time. .......

5 Dorothy has developed a range of attractive insect houses. .......

6 The writer believes that stick insects are the worst possible pets for busy people. .......

7 Dorothy and Naomi had to learn new skills before starting their businesses. .......

8 According to the article, a successful idea has to be a new idea. .......

9 The writer suggests that all hobbies provide opportunities to make money. .......

10 Teens who have achieved something similar are invited to write about it. .......

## 4 Match the highlighted words in the article to the meanings.

1 buying and selling goods through the post .........................

2 taking care of someone or something .........................

3 going to have a baby .........................

4 think carefully about something .........................

## EP Word profile *place*

### Match the sentences to the replies.

1 Where did our team come in the competition? .......

2 Did you get the tickets? .......

3 When is swimming practice this term? .......

4 Can I sit down now? .......

5 Mum's taking me to school early tomorrow. .......

6 I'm excited about Friday – are you? .......

7 Can you save me a place near you on the bus tomorrow? .......

a No, there were no places left by the time I got there. Sorry.

b Ah! So that you can get a place on the theatre trip!

c Am I!? The end-of-year dance is finally taking place! It's going to be awesome!

d Yes, of course. Everyone can return to their places.

e Sure! I'll put my bag on the seat!

f We got second place! I'm really pleased.

g I think it takes place on Mondays.

## SUCCESS WITH ANIMALS

*What do you dream of doing in life? Perhaps you have already achieved some amazing things and have your own success story. Or maybe you just want to be inspired. We spoke to two people who made a name for themselves when they were teenagers.*

One of these successful young businesswomen is Naomi, who began breeding guinea pigs when she was a child, that is, producing baby guinea pigs. She told me that she had bought a female guinea pig from a pet shop and the woman there told her that the guinea pig was probably pregnant. She said she would buy back any babies when they were six to eight weeks old. She said, 'My parents gave me some money to buy more cages, and my brother, who was 10 at the time, went into business with me immediately.' Naomi still sells her baby guinea pigs, but their cages and other equipment are quite expensive, so she has had to learn how to run a business, which she does in the evenings after school.

Another teen who became successful with animals is Dorothy. She began her business at the age of 14, selling stick insect eggs by mail order. Today she is Great Britain's largest breeder of stick insects. Her company sells over 50,000 eggs a year! She studied biology at university to increase her knowledge about these insects. She has even designed special insect houses which are also beautiful to have in the home.

With this knowledge, she is now able to provide her customers with everything they need for their stick insects. If you ask me, stick insects are the perfect pet for the 21st century. These days so many people work all day but they want a pet. Cats and dogs need looking after a lot whereas insects don't. What a great idea!

Since these young teens began their businesses they have had to learn all about managing money, quality control and all the responsibility of a running a small business. It all seems very simple. The secret is to find something that nobody else is doing. But what do you have to do to get started?

Make a list of all your ideas – think about what you want to achieve in the next five years. Do you want to earn money to pay for college, for example? Or do you want to travel the world? Then think about what you need to do this. And finally, consider what you do in your free time – Dorothy and Naomi both made money from their hobbies. Could you develop an interest that would make you some money? Perhaps we will read about your story here one day!

*If you have a success story, email me at jasontalkstosuccess@ourmag.com*

## GRAMMAR   Verbs with two objects

**1** Add *to* or *for* in the correct place in these sentences.

**0** I sent the text ⌄ the wrong person.   ....to....

**1** Stephanie wrote a letter the newspaper.   ............

**2** Mum bought a book of poetry me.   ............

**3** The boys gave a big box of chocolates their father.   ............

**4** Alina and Margie showed their holiday photos their friends.   ............

**5** The grandparents told a story their grandchildren every night.   ............

**2** Write the words in the correct order to make sentences.

**1** secret / best friend / me / My / told / a

.........................................................

**2** surprise present / gave / My / me / a / parents

.........................................................

**3** showed / us / Mum / new dress / her / to

.........................................................

**4** new shoes / bought / Mum / me / a pair / of

.........................................................

**5** sent / a book / to / Mark / his / parents

.........................................................

**6** The teacher / wrote / the parents / a letter / to

.........................................................

**3** Read the text and answer the questions in full.

It was Sara's birthday and she woke up early to see that her phone had been busy through the night! Lots of friends had sent her birthday wishes. As she went downstairs she heard Mum and Dad talking softly and then she saw a huge box in front of them. Dad looked at her and said 'Happy Birthday Sara. Here's your present.' She had no idea what it was. She opened each layer of paper and there was another box, and another box. Finally, she got to the bottom – an envelope with a stamp on it. It was from her grandmother in Australia. As she opened it she saw the words 'London–Sydney' – it was a plane ticket! She couldn't believe it! Mum told her the story – how they had planned it in secret. It was the best present ever. They took a photo and sent it immediately to Grandma.

**1** What had her friends sent her?

.........................................................

**2** What did her parents give her?

.........................................................

**3** Who had sent her the envelope?

.........................................................

**4** Who told her the story?

.........................................................

**5** What did they do in the end?

.........................................................

**4** Complete the second sentence in each pair so that it means the same as the first.

**1** They brought a small present for me.
They brought me .........................................

**2** Josh gave a party invitation to Lucy.
Josh .........................................................

**3** Mr Digby sent his students an email.
Mr Digby ...................................................

**4** Jason took the girl some flowers.
Jason ........................................................

**5** Millie showed the picture to her friends.
Millie.........................................................

**6** The class gave the boy a prize.
The class ...................................................

**5** Correct the mistakes in these sentences or put a tick (✓) by any you think are correct.

**1** I want to introduce you all my friends.

.............................

**2** I tell to her all my secrets.   ............................

**3** She lent the money and then started talking to him.   ............................

**4** When she arrived at school, all her classmates sang 'Happy birthday to you' and they gave to her a lot of presents.   ............................

**5** Together we baked some cakes to our boyfriends.

.............................

## VOCABULARY   Phrasal verbs

**1** Choose the correct prepositions.

**1** Do you believe *in* / *for* luck?

**2** I don't know if I can go to the party – it depends *with* / *on* what my parents say.

**3** Our teacher is busy at the moment because he has to deal *in* / *with* the other biology class.

**4** I'm going to go *in* / *for* that babysitting job.

**5** Harry never joins *into* / *in* sports games.

**6** Maggie got *for* / *onto* the school tennis team!

**2** Complete the text with the correct form of the verbs from the box.

believe   deal   get   go   join

**NATIONAL TEAM SELECTION!**
Congratulations to Harry Rowe and Jessica Ambleside! We always ¹ ........................... in you and now you have both ² ........................... into the national basketball teams. We are very proud of you. We know that you will have to practise a lot and that you will have to ³ ........................... with a lot of pressure. We hope that you will still be able to ⁴ ........................... in regular school activities. Just ⁵ ........................... for it and have fun!

# LISTENING

**1** ▶12 **You will hear a conversation between two teens talking about an idea for a business. Tick (✔) the topics they mention.**

what the business is ☐
managing the product ☐
how they had the idea for the product ☐
what the product is ☐
similar products available ☐
their friends' opinions ☐

**2** ▶12 **Listen again to the first part of the conversation and fill in the missing words.**

**Craig:** So, Kathy, what do you think about
¹ ............................. up our own business?

**Kathy:** I'm not sure. Do you think that our fruit juices are *that* good?

**Craig:** Everyone at school ² ............................. them and you said that your parents really liked them. I think we have a great idea, and ³ ............................. else has done it. A fruit juice in a bag!

**Kathy:** I know, Craig, but that was only because we didn't have any paper cups ⁴ .............................! But that's how all the great ideas start, isn't it? People make a ⁵ ............................. for themselves with crazy ideas! What should we call them? Bag of fruit? Fruit in a bag?

**3** **Answer the questions.**

1 What is the product?
.................................................................

2 Who likes it?
.................................................................

3 How did they get the idea?
.................................................................

4 What are they going to call it?
.................................................................

## EXAM TIPS

**Listening Part 4**
- Read the sentences carefully before you listen, checking which speaker each sentence is about.
- Listen for words or phrases that mean the same as the important words in the sentences.
- Listen for words and phrases that tell you about the speakers' attitude.

**4** ▶12 ⬤ **Look at the six sentences. Listen to the whole conversation and decide if each sentence is correct or incorrect. If it is correct, choose the letter A. If it is not correct, choose the letter B.**

|  | YES | NO |
|---|---|---|
| 1 Craig believes that they have an unusual idea. | A | B |
| 2 Kathy thinks they may become famous. | A | B |
| 3 Craig and Kathy agree to put their idea on social media sites. | A | B |
| 4 Craig suggests all the photos should be taken indoors. | A | B |
| 5 Kathy thinks people will enjoy the product in many places. | A | B |
| 6 Craig thinks that they should only show beautiful people in their advertising. | A | B |

# Acknowledgements

Development of this publication has made use of the Cambridge English Corpus, a multi-billion word collection of spoken and written English. It includes the Cambridge Learner Corpus, a unique collection of candidate exam answers. Cambridge University Press has built up the Cambridge English Corpus to provide evidence about language use that helps to produce better language teaching materials.

This product is informed by English Profile, a Council of Europe-endorsed research programme that is providing detailed information about the language that learners of English know and use at each level of the Common European Framework of Reference (CEFR). For more information, please visit www.englishprofile.org

**The authors and publishers acknowledge the following sources of copyright material and are grateful for the permissions granted. While every effort has been made, it has not always been possible to identify the sources of all the material used, or to trace all copyright holders. If any omissions are brought to our notice, we will be happy to include the appropriate acknowledgements on reprinting.**

Mail Online for the adapted extract on p. 45 'The World's Biggest School' by Daily Mail Reporter, *Mail Online* 23/8/2013; Claire Gournley for the adapted extract on p. 57 from text appearing on her website 'itsmyturntocooktonight.com'. Reproduced by permission of Claire Gournley; First News for the adapted extract on p. 62 'How much time do you spend outside?' by First News Reporter, *First News* 11/04/2014; United Church of God for the adapted extract on p. 81 'Teenage stories: yours could start today,' by Kae Tattersall, *The Good News*.

**Photo acknowledgements**

p. 5: (L) M. Sobreira/Alamy, (R) Pixellover RM 5/Alamy, p. 9: Graham Oliver/Juice Images Corbis, p. 10: Kevin Dodge/ Blend Images/Corbis, p. 13: Pier Marco Tacca/Getty, pp. 25: (L) AlexRoz/Shutterstock, (R) Rodrigo Bellizzi/Shutterstock, p. 27: Iain Masterton/Alamy, p. 29: Photopat vintage/Alamy, p. 30: Bernhard Lang/Getty, pp. 33: (L) UrbanImages/Alamy, (C) Heritage Images/Getty, (R) Sergey Parantaev/Alamy, pp. 39: (T) Serhiy Kobyakov/Shutterstock, (C) irawatfoto/ Shutterstock, (B) Anton Starikov/Alamy, pp. 40: (TL) Gillmar/ Shutterstock, (TR) Suzanne Long/Alamy , (CL) EMprize/ Shutterstock, (CR) Henrik Winther Andersen/Alamy, (BL) CountrySideCollection/Homer Sykes/Alamy, (BR) Momanuma/ Shutterstock, (R) Kevin Schafer/Getty, p. 41: Mangostock/ Shutterstock, pp. 43: (L) Gallo Images/Alamy, (TR) JLImages/ Alamy, (BR) FloridaStock/Shutterstock, p. 45: STRDEL/ Stringer/Getty, p. 49: Filip Fuxa/Shutterstock, p. 51: S.Borisov/ Shutterstock, p. 53: AF archive/Alamy, p. 62: Julia Kuznetsova/ Shutterstock, p. 66: @erics/Shutterstock, p. 69: Fullempty/ Shutterstock, p. 73: Matt Baron/BEI/Rex, p. 77: (T) Robin Bush/ Getty, (B) cmgirl/Shutterstock, p. 81: (T) nico99/Shutterstock, (B) Kosobu/Shutterstock, p. 83: fotohunter/Shutterstock

Front cover photograph by Phase4Studios/Shutterstock.

**Illustrations**

Mark Duffin pp. 15, 34; Stuart Harrison pp. 5, 12, 14, 22, 47, 52, 68, 74; Martin Sanders (Beehive Illustration) p. 17; Alex Sotirovski (Beehive Illustration) pp. 16, 31, 35, 48, 56, 61, 75.

**The publishers are grateful to the following contributors:** text design and layouts: emc design Ltd; cover design: Andrew Ward; picture research: emc design Ltd; audio recordings: produced by IH Sound and recorded at DSound, London; edited by Diane Hall.